Battlefield Walks
NORTHUMBERLAND

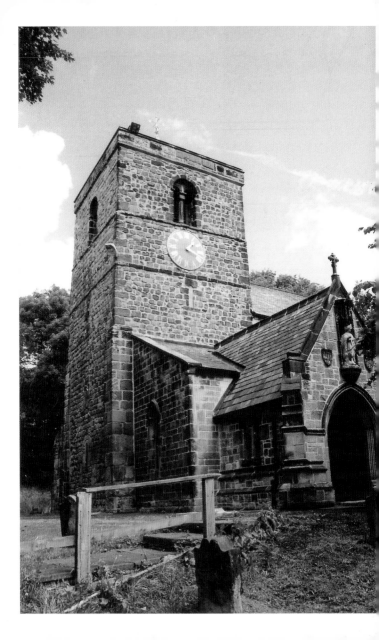

Battlefield Walks
NORTHUMBERLAND

Rupert Matthews

F

FRANCES LINCOLN LIMITED
PUBLISHERS

Frances Lincoln Ltd
4 Torriano Mews
Torriano Avenue
London NW5 2RZ
www.franceslincoln.com

Battlfield Walks: Northumberland
Copyright © Frances Lincoln Ltd 2008
Text, maps and photographs copyright
© Rupert Matthews 2008

First Frances Lincoln edition 2008.

A catalogue record for this book is available from
the British Library.

Printed and bound in China.

ISBN 13: 978-0-7112-2827-6

2 4 6 8 9 7 5 3 1

CONTENTS

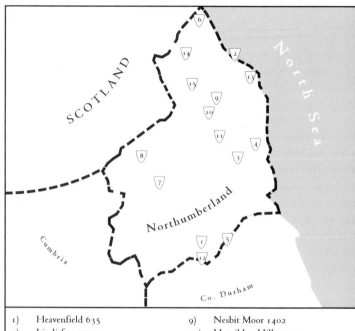

1) Heavenfield 635	9) Nesbit Moor 1402
2) Lindisfarne 793	10) Homildon Hill 1402
3) Battle Bridge 875	11) Hedgeley Moor 1464
4) Alnwick 1093 & 1174	12) Hexham 1464
5) Corbridge 1312	13) Bamburgh Castle 1464
6) Halidon Hill 1333	14) Norham Castle 1513
7) Otterburn 1388	15) Flodden 1513
8) Fulhope Law 1400	

INTRODUCTION

The beautiful county of Northumberland is one of the most scenic in England, and one of the most fought over. It was, of course, the border with Scotland that made this such a violent and warlike county. Time and again, the Scots came south pillaging, looting and killing. Time and again, the northern English rallied to the banners to drive them off. The great noble families of the Percies, Umfravilles and Nevilles led the resistance. Sometimes the Scots were back over the border with their plunder before they could be caught. Other times they were ambushed on their way home, leading to battles unparalleled in ferocity in this island.

Those days of border warfare are some four centuries behind us, but they are not forgotten. Monuments stand on many of the battlefields, and the Percies still live at Alnwick Castle which they held against the invaders many times. But peace now reigns over the borders. In these days of Scottish devolution and, perhaps one day, independence it must be hoped that the Scots do not come raiding again. Northumberland has battlefields enough and does not need any more.

This book takes the reader on a journey through the military history of the county. It looks at fifteen of the more important battles and sieges to be fought out here, putting them in their historic context and explaining how and why the battles were fought. The book looks at the developing weaponry and tactical face of warfare and how this affected the decisions of the commanders and the outcome of the struggles.

Each battle is described in the course of a walk around the battlefield. Generally, though not always, the walk follows the route followed by one commander or unit during the battle. The text describes the route to be taken, and where to pause to inspect the points where actions took place and events happened. All the routes have been walked by the author.

Sadly, not all the battlefields of Northumberland can be traced out on the ground. The famous Redewire Fray of 1575, for instance, took place on bleak, windswept moorland high up in the Cheviots where no modern footpaths are to be found. The scene can, however, be viewed from the layby on the A697 at Carter Bar. The siege of Morpeth Castle and the attendant skirmishes were fought over ground on which now stands the town of Morpeth itself – though the castle is worth a visit. And several of the Dark Age battles are mere names, the sites of which cannot even be guessed at.

Even when the site of a battle is known for certain, problems still remain. The men fighting the battles had more important things to do than take careful notes about times and locations of individual events. All too often historical records are rather vague as to exactly where or when something happened. In writing this book I have tried hard to locate events on the ground as best I can. In the text I point out when a fact is known for certain, when it is probable and when it is merely conjectural. The maps of the battles should be viewed with this in mind.

This book has been a joy to research and to write. I must thank the good people of Northumberland for the warm welcomes that they extended to me during my visits to the places mentioned, and express appreciation for the research facilities available in the county. I would also like to thank my wife for her patience.

1. HEAVENFIELD
635

Distance:	½ mile.
Terrain:	A fairly gentle walk over exposed hillsides where the surfaces can be uneven. It is a rewarding walk that explores one of the most important battlefields of Dark Age Britain.
Public Transport:	Tyne Valley Coaches route 888 from Hexham to Humshaugh, stopping at the crossroads of the A6079 and B6318. From this stop walk half a mile east along the B6318 to join the walk at Point 1.
Parking:	A small layby on the B6318 beside the battle monument, where the walk starts and finishes.
Refreshments:	No shops or pubs along the route of the walk.

After the Roman Empire crumbled in the fifth century the province of Britain was left to look after its own defences. For a while the Romano-Britons maintained the administration and culture of the Romans, but eventually invaders from outside and internal disputes caused a collapse. By the early seventh century most of southern lowland was in the hands of the English while the Britons held on to Cornwall, Cumbria and Wales. The fate of northern Britain was in the balance. The Battle of Heavenfield tipped that balance decisively and for ever.

The northern English were divided into two kingdoms. Deira centred on the fertile lands north of the Humber and Bernicia with its impregnable stronghold of Bamburgh. The two kingdoms often co-operated, when they were known collectively as Northumbria. The Britons, or Welsh, were even more fragmented.

However in 632 Cadwallon, Prince of Gwynedd in northern Wales bound the northern Britons together more or less willingly into a grand alliance. He marched into Northumbria and killed King Edwin of Bernicia at the Battle of Hatfield Chase. King Eanfrith of Deira hurried to make peace, offering tribute to Cadwallon, but the British leader had him executed out of hand. Cadwallon marched through the English lands, demanding instant submission and heavy payments of tribute, killing any who resisted. Confident that he had imposed his rule on the English, Cadwallon went home in the autumn of 632 to concentrate on cementing his power among his various allies.

In the spring of 635, we don't know the exact date, young Oswald, the brother of King Eanfrith, came out of hiding. He declared that he was King of Deira and would pay no tribute to Cadwallon. The English flocked to join their dashing young king, but Cadwallon moved just as swiftly. He led an army out of Wales, pushed north through Cumbria to pick up allied troops, then marched up Liddesdale. Perhaps he hoped to attract allies from the Britons living in Galloway and Dumfries. At any rate, he turned south near Ricarton and so reached the upper end of the Tyne Valley from where he could strike into the English lands.

Oswald knew Cadwallon was coming and sent out orders to his supporters to muster just north of Hexham where a milecastle stood on Hadrian's Wall. When the banners of Cadwallon came in sight approaching from the north, Oswald's army was not yet complete and the English were heavily outnumbered. Despite this, Oswald chose to fight.

THE WALK

1. From the layby on the B6318, signposted for the battle monument, enter the field via the gate, then turn left along

The large wooden cross that identifies the layby where the walk starts and finishes.

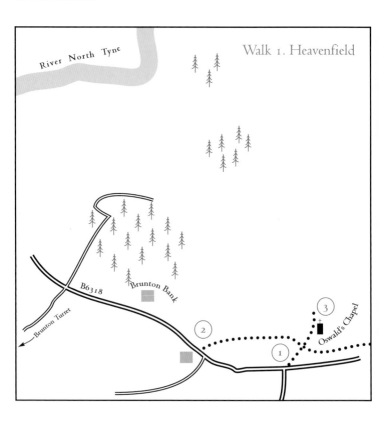

the Hadrian's Wall Walk. Climb over a stile, then follow the
walk downhill, over a second stile and into an open field.
Continue along the Hadrian's Wall walk to the site of a
milecastle beside a modern gate. Although it played no role
in the battle, there is rather more to see at the Brunton
Turret, about 800 yards further along the Hadrian's Wall
Walk. If you wish to see something of the Roman wall, you
should continue along the signposted walk to the turret,
then return.

The stile by which the walk leaves the first field to enter a patch of woodland.

The site of the milecastle. Nothing now remains above ground, but the small fortress stood just to the right of the gate through the hedge to the road.

△ The Brunton turret and an adjacent
stretch of Hadrian's Wall. The wall
stands about 4 feet tall here, but was
originally over 20 feet tall.

▷ The route of Oswald's advance to
battle goes uphill through some woods to
reach the bare hilltop where he was to
launch a charge against the invaders.

An English warrior from the time of Heavenfield. He carries a long, heavy spear and a round shield, the basic equipment of any English fighter at this time. He also carries a sword so he is most likely a wealthier landowner.

Today the scene is one of empty grazing land and small woods, but in 635 it was very different. Hadrian's Wall dominated the scene. It was more than two hundred years since the wall had seen any maintenance work and it was no doubt out of repair. The battlements must have collapsed by this time, but the main wall itself was intact and formed a significant obstacle. The milecastle had a watchtower and a gate through the wall. No doubt Cadwallon was heading for this gate to get his army and its supply train past the wall, but Oswald had beaten him to it. As the Britons came over the crest of the hill they will have seen the English drawn up for battle in front of the milecastle.

Exactly what happened next is not entirely clear from the sources. Oswald was clearly in position first, having drawn his army up for divine service at dawn. It is likely that the king and his entourage were sleeping in the milecastle, and that the army was camped on the level ground around it. A priest, probably from the church at Hexham, had brought along a large wooden

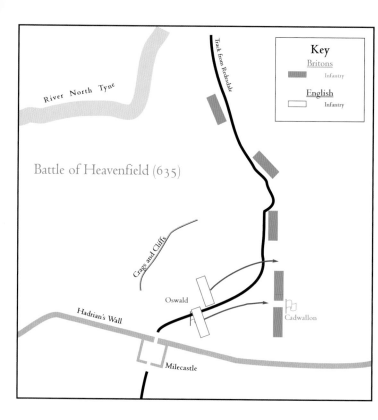

cross. Oswald himself held up this cross and ordered his army 'Let us all kneel together and ask the true and living God Almighty of His mercy to protect us from the arrogant savagery of our enemies since He knows that we fight in a just cause to save our nation.'

The prayers over, the English formed up and advanced. The usual English tactic at this time was the shieldwall. The army was drawn up in a dense mass some eight or ten men deep with the most experienced and best equipped men at the front. These men

The route of the English charge across the open hilltop that would become known as Heavenfield. The combined invading army was about where the chapel now stands when the English force made contact.

Looking north from the chapel along the route by which Cadwallon and his army advanced.

St Oswald's Chapel is now one of three churches within the parish and is now popular for weddings.

interlocked their shields to form a solid wall. Like the Britons, most men had a large round shield and thrusting spear, though many of those in the front rank would also have had a sword. The front two or three ranks of men could reach the enemy with their spears, those behind providing replacements as men fell dead or stepped back wounded.

The shieldwall was an effective tactic, but it depended entirely on the men keeping tight formation. That Oswald chose to advance shows that he had great faith in his front rank to keep position as they walked, then jogged forward.

2. **Return back along the path to the first field. This was the route taken by Oswald and his army as they advanced from the milecastle to face Cadwallon. Once in the field, bear left**

to reach the stone wall left of the chapel. Look out over the hillside in front of you. An overgrown and barely used footpath goes down the hill into the valley to the north.

In 635 this path was a track used by drovers to bring their livestock down from the upland summer pastures in autumn. It was along this route that Cadwallon and his army advanced to battle. The Britons had camped somewhere near Chollerton and set out at dawn. It was perhaps only an hour after dawn when they reached this spot.

At this date British armies were primarily made up of infantry. Some men would have ridden mountain ponies on campaign, but they seem to have fought on foot. Each man carried a round wooden shield some 3 feet or so in diameter that was painted with bright designs. The main offensive weapon was an eight or 9-foot spear with a heavy iron head that was used in a thrusting fashion. Only the richer men had helmets of iron or shirts of mail or toughened leather.

We do know that Cadwallon had an impressive battle standard, based on that of the later Roman cavalry. It resembled a modern windsock in shape, the tail being of golden silk and the head taking the form of a gilded bronze dragon's head and forequarters.

As he advanced Cadwallon will have known that Oswald and his men were somewhere in the area, but the British do not seem to have realised just how close the enemy were.

Cadwallon's army had been marching in a column up the hillside. It seems most likely that only the forward units had got on to the hilltop and formed up when the English attacked. This would explain the fact that the English charge was successful in breaking up the British army into fragments.

The fighting was short, but apparently very bloody. The

British stood firm for a while, hoping that the rest of their army would have time to climb the hill to come to their aid. It was not to be. The British formation crumpled and broke up. Cadwallon himself was caught on the wrong side of the surging English formation. Much of his army was to the north of Oswald's men, but Cadwallon was to the south. Realising the battle was lost, Cadwallon fled.

Oswald set up the large wooden cross on the spot where he won the battle. About sixty years later the priests of Hexham erected a small stone chapel beside the rotting cross. The small chapel to be seen today was erected in 1737 on the site.

3. Visit the chapel, which has an interesting little exhibition about the battle and Oswald's reign. There are fragmentary remains of the earlier chapel preserved here. The chapel has a small box for contributions to maintaining the exhibition, which should be supported.

This marks the end of the walk, but it is possible to continue the route by car. Drive to Hexham, then head south-east on the B6306. As this road leaves Hexham, turn right on to the lane signposted to Ordley, which roughly follows the route of the old Roman road along which Cadwallon fled. A mile beyond Ordley the lane crosses a small stream, the Rowley Burn. It was here that the pursuing English caught up with Cadwallon and killed him.

The battlefield became known as Heavenfield in tribute to the cross erected by Oswald. The death of Cadwallon destroyed the alliance of British states that he had created before it had a chance to become a permanent fixture. Oswald used his new prestige as a heroic king to take over Bernicia, creating a unified English kingdom of Northumbria that had the economic and military strength to become the dominant power north of the Humber.

In this field, south of the modern road, a number of skulls and other human bones were discovered a few years ago. They are presumed to have been the remains of warriors killed in the battle.

Within a generation all the lands from the Humber to the Forth were English. Only the mountains of Cumbria held out against the invaders, and they would fall soon after.

The Battle of Heavenfield ensured that northern England became English, not Welsh.

2. LINDISFARNE
793

Distance:	3¼ miles.
Terrain:	A gentle walk over flat ground, largely over footpaths, with one stretch over a lane.
Public Transport:	Travelsure route 477 from Berwick to Holy Island is dependent on the tides, so check before travelling.
Parking:	A car park on the access road from the causeway to the village. The island is accessible only at low tide, so check the tide times with Tourist Information before setting out.
Refreshments:	Two pubs serving meals and one shop selling snacks in the village as well as a couple of cafés.

With hindsight it was clear that trouble had been brewing for some years. The Shetlands and Orkneys had both been overrun by Viking invaders in the later eighth century, while both Caithness and Sutherland in Scotland had been attacked and pillaged. In 789 three ships from Scandinavia put in to Portland on the south coast of England. When the local government official rode down to ask the new arrivals their business, they killed him and then fled.

Even so the people of Northumberland do not seem to have expected any trouble. They certainly took no precautions. They later said that mysterious fiery dragons had been seen in the sky and regarded these as omens of evil. Whether these were comets, meteorites of mere imagination it is impossible to know.

In fact the North Sea was already being travelled by compara-tively large fleets of Norwegians intent on exploration, loot and violence. Whether it was pressure of population increase at home, a thirst for adventure or pagan savagery that urged the Vikings on is still an open question, but come they did. They were pagans who

The gaunt ruins of the medieval Lindisfarne Priory. The island has long been known as Holy Isle because of its links to the Christian religion, and especially to the monks who introduced the faith to these lands. The ruins to be seen today date to some centuries after the sacking of Lindisfarne by the Vikings.

A Viking warrior. He carries a pair of throwing javelins with which to assault the enemy before close combat is joined. His main weapon is a battleaxe, with a short sword for back up. He has a metal helmet and chain shirt as well as an iron-bound wooden shield, so he is well armoured for his time.

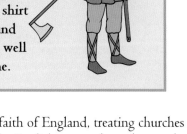

cared nothing for the Christian faith of England, treating churches with a contempt that shocked the English – or at least the monks who wrote down records of events.

The bulk of the English were probably more worried by Viking prowess in battle. In terms of technology the Vikings had little to make them superior to the English. Both nations fought on foot using round shields and spears as their main weapons. Richer men could afford helmets or mail shirts, and swords were prized by those who could afford them.

In battle the Vikings used shieldwall tactics similar to the English, though with a few refinements. It is true that the Vikings that came to England were the tough young men who had trained for war and so were generally better at fighting that the average English farmer called from his plough to fight, but a good Englishman was the equal of a good Viking.

What made the Vikings really difficult to counter was their mobility. They travelled in fast, sleek ships that could carry them quickly along coasts or up rivers. They would attack one area, looting it thoroughly and quickly. As soon as the English mustered an army to fight, the Vikings leapt back to their ships and fled, only to search for a new unprotected area to attack.

The first taste the English had of this awesome new force came at Lindisfarne, then the seat of one of the oldest and most respected monasteries in Britain.

The Vikings were nothing if not thorough when it came to killing. They left so few survivors – if any – on Lindisfarne that it is very difficult to reconstruct the events of 8 January 793 with any real certainty, though the outline of events is clear enough.

THE WALK

1. Make your way to the ruined priory that lies in the centre of Holy Island village, off Fenkle Street.

The ruins to be seen today date to the medieval period. The monastery was founded in 1093 by monks from Durham on the site of the original Lindisfarne Monastery, which had been founded in 634. Of the establishment that stood here in 793 nothing remains except a few inscribed stones carefully stored in museums. It is most likely that the monastery of 793 consisted of a small stone church, located just east of the modern parish church, surrounded by a number of wooden or stone huts that did service as bedrooms, workshops and library. There may have been around thirty monks, plus a hundred or so staff, servants and workmen.

2. Leave the ruins and head east along Marygate to join the track signposted to the castle. Follow the track to the castle.

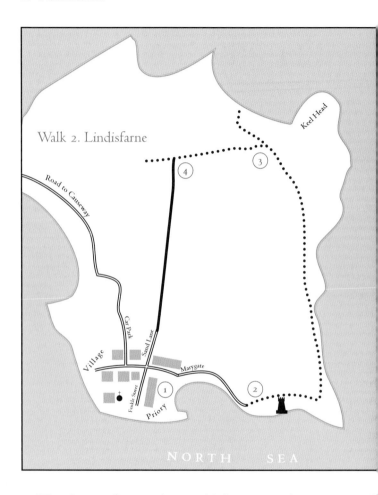

Walk 2. Lindisfarne

Road to Causeway

Keel Head

Village

Car Park

Sand Lane

Fenkle Street

Marygate

Priory

NORTH SEA

This famous fortress dates to Tudor times, when Henry VIII established it as a springboard for military operations against the Scots. It was abandoned when King James VI of Scotland became James I of England in 1603 and it fell into ruin. The empty shell was restored in 1903 by Sir Edwin Lutyens. In 793 there was

The parish church on Lindisfarne was built in 1140, though much altered in the thiteenth century. Unlike the monastery it remains intact and contains some fascinating statues and monuments.

nothing on this dramatic crag, except presumably a few sheep. They took no notice of the long-hulled ships that came nosing down from the north soon after dawn on 8 January.

3. From the castle continue along the footpath as it runs first east, then north along the shoreline and past a pond. A hundred yards or so north of the pond the path turns left while a second path runs off to the right down to the beach at Keel Head.

It was almost certainly here that the Viking ships beached. They had been coming down from the Viking settlements in Sutherland and were aware that a monastery stood on the island. Monasteries were known to house valuable treasuries and to be devoid of fighting men, making them tempting targets for raiders.

The ships were designed to be hauled ashore, and the shelving beach here was ideal. Once the ships had grounded, the warriors

△ Seen from the monastery ruins, Lindisfarne Castle looms up atop its remote crag on the far side of the harbour.

◁ A striking statue of St Aiden, founder of the Christian community on Lindisfarne in 635, stands outside the parish church.

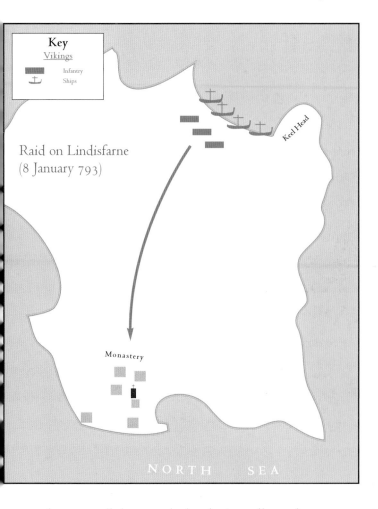

Key
Vikings

Infantry
Ships

Raid on Lindisfarne
(8 January 793)

Keel Head

Monastery

N O R T H   S E A

swarmed out to pull them up the beach. A small guard was put to watch the ships, just in case of trouble, while most of the men raced south towards the distant monastic buildings visible over the smooth turf.

The lane back to the village from the northern beach runs past these farm buildings.

4. Return to the main path, following it west for a short distance before taking a surfaced track heading directly south along the route taken by the Vikings. The track emerges back into the village at Sand Lane, which continues over Marygate to return to the ruins and so end the walk.

Once at the monastery, the Vikings wasted little time killing everybody they could find. Anything of value was stolen and the buildings set on fire. The destruction was dreadful, but not complete. A few monks survived the raid – though perhaps only because they were not on the island at the time. They patched up the church and rebuilt the living quarters but the monastery never really regained its former splendor.

The Vikings, meanwhile, returned north and did not come back to England for more than a decade. The raids grew in frequency and size as the years passed. In 875 a massive Viking fleet and army returned to Northumbria. The monks abandoned the island and moved by a circuitous route to Durham, where they established the cathedral that still dominates that city.

3. BATTLE BRIDGE
875

Distance:	2½ miles.
Terrain:	This gentle walk over relatively undemanding countryside is largely over surfaced lanes, though one long section goes over open fields.
Public Transport:	No regular public transport routes serving this walk.
Parking:	A small layby immediately west of Battle Bridge, where the walk starts and finishes.
Refreshments:	No shops or pubs along the route of the walk.

The ninth century was a harsh time for Northumberland. The Vikings were at their most active at this time. Several bands of pagan raiders came over the North Sea to loot and pillage the countryside, combining into large armies whenever resistance materialised, then scattering again to steal everything they could when no English armies were nearby.

In 867 Ivar the Boneless, the leading Viking leader, crushed a Northumbrian army, killed the English king and set up an obscure nobleman named Egbert to be the puppet ruler of Northumbria. In 873 Egbert died, whereupon the Northumbrian nobles elected a man named Ricsige and declared that no more tribute would be paid to the Vikings. Ivar was by this date dead, his place taken by his brother Halfdan who was busy fighting in southern England. Once a truce had been arranged, and tribute gained, in the south, Halfdan ordered the Viking army back north to crush the Northumbrians. Half the Viking army refused to obey, preferring to pillage East Anglia instead. Nevertheless, Halfdan arrived in the Tyne in the spring of 875 with a sizeable army, perhaps some 10,000 strong.

▷ The layby where the walk begins is opposite this old signpost. It is the only secure parking place available on theses lanes.

▽ Battlebridge Farm seen from the layby. The records of the battle are fragmentary, but it seems likely that the English commander took up station on the ridge that links the farm and the layby as this would have given him fine views east, the direction from which the Vikings were advancing.

King Ricsige decided against facing the fearsome Vikings in open battle, preferring instead to wage a war of raid, ambush and skirmish. His key aim appears to have been to deny either food or money to the Vikings. Ricsige knew the Vikings were after loot and hoped that they would not stay in Northumbria long if they did not get much of it. Food was just as important to a raiding Viking force, so Ricsige ordered his subjects to hide all food stores and drive their cattle into the dense forests and high mountains of Northumberland.

Halfdan countered by dividing his force and sending them deep into the Northumberland interior with orders to find and kill Ricsige, while gathering as much food and loot as possible. Sometime in the summer of 875, the date has been lost, one force of Vikings rowed their ships up the coast to the Aln, beached their ships at Alnmouth and marched up the river.

The details of the subsequent battle have been lost for the simple fact that almost nobody survived the slaughter to tell the tale. We do not even know the names of the rival commanders. Nevertheless, the outline of events can be traced fairly accurately.

THE WALK

1. From the layby you can follow a footpath to Battle Bridge Farm if you wish. Then return to the layby. Head north along the lane beside the layby. Turn right along a bridleway that runs between two fences and beside a wet ditch. Follow this path to the Edlingham Burn and cross it by means of a modern foot-bridge. Beyond the bridge pass through a small wood, then emerge into open pastureland.

The fields hereabouts are marked by the signs of what lies beneath. These fields were the site of a flourishing village in early

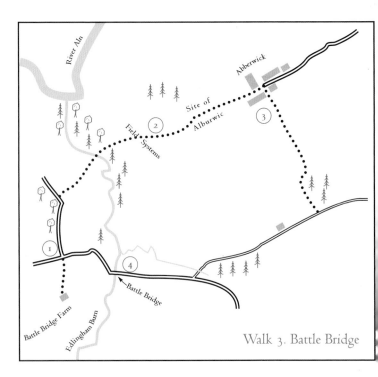

Walk 3. Battle Bridge

medieval times. In 875 it was a busy and large settlement named Alburwic, much larger than the modern Abberwick which has taken its name. It seems to have been an administrative centre of some kind, and was certainly the focus for what was to follow.

You will notice a series of long, low parallel humps in the first field that you cross. These are the remains of the communal field systems favoured by the early English. In most places they have been destroyed by subsequent ploughing, but here they have not been ploughed under as the land has been given over to pasture. In the second large field the humps are less regular and larger, covering as they do the ruins of the village itself.

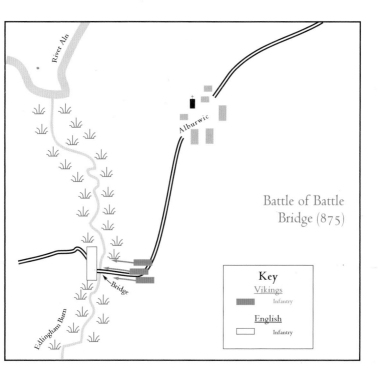

The Battle of Battle Bridge (875) map, showing the River Aln, Edlingham Burn, the Bridge, Alburwic, and positions of Viking and English infantry.

Key
Vikings
Infantry
English
Infantry

When the local English realised that a Viking force was coming up the valley they decided to fight. Why they ignored the clear orders of their king is unknown. Perhaps they were unable to get their produce and livestock away in time, perhaps they thought they could cope with a small detachment of the pagan invaders. For whatever reason a force of local men was mustered. Whoever commanded these men knew that Alburwic itself could not easily be defended. He moved his little army west.

2. Continue along the footpath to reach modern Abberwick. Pass to the right of barns and other farm buildings. Then turn

△ Left: The walk leaves the surfaced lane at this signpost and heads east beside a ditch to enter woodland on the far side of a pasture field. Right: The modern footbridge that carries the walk over the stream and into a patch of woodland.

▽ The cattle ford beside the footbridge. At the time of the battle fords such as this would have been of use to travellers, but would not have offered travelling armies a secure crossing – especially not if the raiders were loaded down with plunder.

right through a five bar gate. Continue straight on through a few trees to enter an open field. Climb up this field, keeping a hedge to your left. Thereafter follow the signs for the public footpath that goes over the hill to reach a lane beyond. At the lane turn right and walk down hill. At a T-junciton turn right and very soon reach a stream.

This stream is, again, the Edlingham Burn. In 875 it was broader than today and edged by a belt of marshland. The only practical crossing was here, where the modern road crosses the stream. The English commander decided to hold this crossing point. He would have known that the advancing Vikings had to come this way as they moved up the south bank of the Aln and must have thought he could halt them.

He was wrong.

At this date the English armies were little altered in terms of equipment from that of the Battle of Heavenfield. Rather more men would have been able to afford mail jackets and helmets, but the main weapons remained shield and spear, backed up by swords. As a hastily raised local force, the army mustering on the banks of the Edlingham Burn would have been composed mostly of local farmers and workmen. Such men were strong and brave, but simply did not have the time to spend training in the skills needed to hold the tight formation needed if a shieldwall was to be effective in battle.

The approaching Vikings were very different. These men had been fighting and looting around England for some years. They had the money to afford quality armour and weaponry. Moreover they were highly experienced and accustomed to working together. In terms of equipment they were not very different from the better-equipped Englishmen. They wore mail shirts, carried round shields and relied on spear and sword in combat. One key difference was

The site of the lost village, marked by bumps and dips in the ground, with the modern farm beyond. The walk crosses this field, then passes to the right of the farm buildings.

that many Vikings carried an axe. Some axes were not much larger than a modern timber axe, but some were truly monstrous weapons with cutting edges 14 inches across and handles 6 feet long. Such an axe could slice a man in half with ease.

In terms of tactics, the Vikings also favoured the shieldwall, but had refined its use. They often formed up with a triangular bulge forward from the front of the shieldwall. This served to punch a hole through an enemy shieldwall and disrupt its formation.

The main fighting took place in and around the stream. In 875 there was probably a narrow wooden bridge over the stream itself. The Vikings may have waded over the marshes to outflank the English, or they may simply have stormed forward over the bridge relying on their skills to defeat the enemy.

However the Vikings got over the Edlingham Burn, they certainly did get across the stream. The English formation rapidly broke up as the poorly trained locals were overwhelmed by the

The view from the hill above Abberwick Farm. The advancing Vikings were marching up the valley of the Aln on a plunder raid. They probably did not expect to meet any real resistance as they crested this slope, and were in for a nasty surprise.

disciplined Vikings. The battle became first a rout and then a slaughter. Only a handful of the English got away.

The fight at what was soon named Battle Bridge may have been a disaster for the local English, but it was perversely hugely beneficial for King Ricsige and Northumbria more generally. With the awful fate of the men of Alburwic to guide them, the Northumbrians fell in with the plans and orders of their king.

The war saw no more major battles, but instead a long drawn out campaign of guerrilla actions, cat-and-mouse raids and hunts for food. By the spring of 866 both Halfdan and Ricsige realised that neither of them could win. They decided to divide the kingdom of Northumbria between them.

Halfdan took the land from the Tees to the Humber. He divided the lands up among his men, effectively creating the land of Yorkshire with its many Scandinavian place names and proud heritage of being slightly separate from the rest of England.

Ricsige kept the lands north of the Tees. The preservation of an independent English kingdom north of the Viking territories was to be of enormous benefit to the English when the fightback under Alfred the Great got underway. Ricsige's successors kept their swords in the Vikings' backs, ensuring that they could never concentrate their full force against the southern English without fear of an attack from the north.

4. Cross the bridge and climb a slope to return to the layby where the walk began.

▷ *The Battle Bridge is a modern construction, but it stands on the site of a medieval forebear. The bridge around which the battle raged was almost certainly within a few feet of the present crossing.*

4. ALNWICK
1093 & 1174

Distance:	4 miles.
Terrain:	This walk encounters no steep hills and is largely over surfaced lanes and tracks. However two sections cross riverside meadows that can be wet even in relatively dry weather.
Public Transport:	There is a train station at Alnmouth, from which a regular bus service runs to Alnwick. National Express route 591 runs to Alnwick from Berwick and the Arriva Northumbria route 518 runs to Alnwick from Newcastle.
Parking:	On-street parking and a car park available in Alnwick.
Refreshments:	Several pubs in Alnwick serving meals and shops selling snacks and soft drinks.

By the eleventh century both England and Scotland had become unified kingdoms, each with a single monarch taking the place of the various princes, earls and kings who had ruled petty states such as Lindsey, Mercia or Dalriada. England was the more united of the two as the rule of the King of Scotland was enforced only sporadically in the Highlands and islands. Nevertheless the formation of two powerful kingdoms was a significant step in the history of Britain. It was, perhaps, inevitable that trouble would eventually flare up between the two kingdoms. When it came, however, it took everyone by surprise. For the outbreak of hostilities was not due to border disputes or feudal intrigue but to a badly timed joke.

In the summer of 1093 King Malcolm III of Scotland travelled south to the court of King William II of England. Malcolm had married an English wife and, through her, owned several estates in England. Under the feudal law of the time

Malcolm was expected to do homage to the King of England for these lands, though Malcolm was careful to ensure that the form of oath did not affect his independence as King of Scotland. The negotiations over exactly what form of oath should be taken had lasted six years, but at last Malcolm was heading south.

The two kings met and got on well, although they were very different men. Malcolm was a talented administrator, devout Christian and devoted family man. William was rash, witty and gay – in both senses of the word. Unfortunately William, after a few drinks, chose to crack a joke at the expense of Malcolm. William and his gay friends thought the jest hugely funny, but Malcolm thought it insulting and obscene. As soon as he could do so without arousing suspicion, he gathered his entourage and returned to Scotland. Once home Malcolm declared war and mustered an army with which to invade England.

The Scottish army marched south in October, plundering its way down the prosperous plains east of the Cheviot Hills. Early in November they reached Alnwick, one of the most powerful castles in Northumberland. Malcolm knew that if the invasion was to continue he had to take Alnwick. He camped his main army north of the Aln on the slopes of the hill overlooking the valley and set to work.

Robert de Mowbray, Earl of Northumberland, was at Bamburgh Castle when the Scots invaded. Malcolm had bypassed the impregnable stronghold, leaving scouts to watch Mowbray and his small force. Lacking in number Mowbray's force may have been but it included some of the most talented and skilled knights of northern England. Mowbray decided to act. He slipped out of Bamburgh and rode quickly towards Alnwick.

The main gates to Alnwick Castle. The walk starts here, moving off to the left of this photo and down the hill to Lion Bridge. The castle has been altered and improved over the years, but this gateway has stood largely unaltered for centuries.

Alnwick Castle seen from Lion Bridge. The current bridge is only about 300 years old, but it stands on the site of the original crossing over the Aln that the castle was intended to guard.

THE WALK

1. **From in front of the main gate of Alnwick Castle head north along the B6341 to cross the River Aln by way of the famous Lion Bridge. Immediately north of the river turn right through a kissing gate and along a footpath that crosses parkland. There are magnificent views of Alnwick Castle to be had from this path. The route passes between two small woods and emerges on to a road. Turn left and follow this lane to a crossroads. Turn left into the lane heading north-west.**

It was at about this spot that Mowbray and his men emerged from the forest that then covered much of the area soon after noon on 13 November. They could scarcely believe their eyes. On the slope to their front was camped the entire Scottish army, sitting down to eat dinner and with no guards posted. Putting their spurs to their horses, the English knights charged.

At this date the mounted knight was the most powerful weapon on the battlefield. Each knight had a long mail shirt that reached to at least the knees and down to the wrists. Some men had mail gauntlets and a few invested in the newly developed mail trousers to protect their legs. The head was covered by a round helmet that had a nasal guard or face mask. Each man carried a large shield that was shaped rather like a kite, the pointed end reaching down to protect the entire left side of the body. Thus dressed the knights were almost impervious to most contemporary weapons.

The weapon of choice was the lance, a wooden shaft about 8 feet long on which was mounted a broad-bladed steel head. This was held couched under the arm so that the entire weight of the charging horse and man could be delivered through the weapon. Most knights had a sword for closequarter combat, though some preferred an axe or mace.

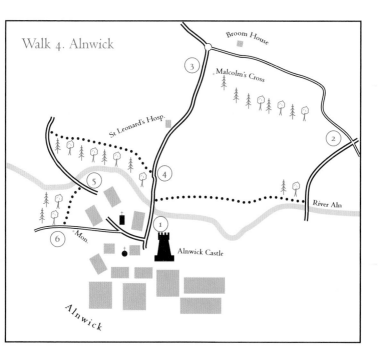

Knights usually formed up three or four ranks deep and rode knee to knee in a compact mass that could simply roll over or crash through any enemy formation that was not tightly formed and well disciplined. Mowbray did not have time to form his men up carefully before charging, but they were all experienced knights and would have known what was expected of them.

2. Continue along the lane, following the route of the English advance. Where the lane passes Broom House the charging knights entered the Scots camp. Turn left at a roundabout, then leave the road through a gate to enter a patch of woodland to find Malcolm's Cross.

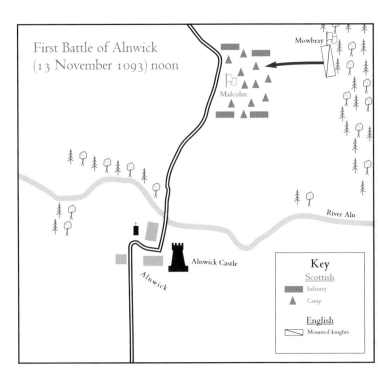

First Battle of Alnwick
(13 November 1093) noon

Mowbray

Malcolm

River Aln

Alnwick Castle

Alnwick

Key

Scottish

Infantry

Camp

English

Mounted knights

This tall stone cross was erected in 1774 by Elizabeth, Duchess of Northumberland and a descendent of King Malcolm. A short distance to the left can be seen the crumbling stump of the medieval monument that it replaced. This marks the spot where King Malcolm tried to rally his scattered and unarmoured men in the face of the English charge. Some men gathered to their king, but most fled down the hill to the west.

An English knight named Hamund was among those who turned to attack the small knot of faithful men. His lance struck King Malcolm, throwing him to the ground and wounding him severely. When their king went down, the Scots

▷ Malcolm's Cross marks the spot where King Malcolm of Scotland was mortally wounded during the First Battle of Alnwick. This is an eighteenth-century construction, the original medieval stump lies hidden in the undergrowth nearby.

▽ After their king was hacked down the Scots fled over these fields to the west in a desperate effort to escape the English knights.

The English-Norman knights who defeated and killed King Malcolm would have been dressed much like this figure. He wears a mail coat down to his knees, with a mail coif under his metal helmet. The long, kite-shaped shield provided protection to his entire left side from shoulder to foot and could also be used to protect the horse. The main offensive weapon in the lance, with a sword for close combat. At Alnwick most fighting was done with the lance as the horsemen first smashed into the Scottish camp and then pursued the fugitives.

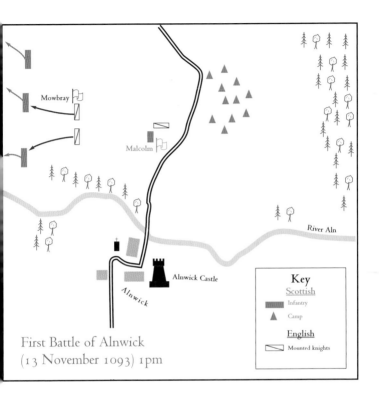

Mowbray

Malcolm

Alnwick Castle

Alnwick

River Aln

Key

Scottish

▓ Infantry

▲ Camp

English

◻ Mounted knights

First Battle of Alnwick
(13 November 1093) 1pm

began edging down the slope carrying their wounded king with them.

3. Return to the road and continue south until the sad ruins of St Leonard's Hospital are found on the right side of the road.

It was at this spot that the Scots realised their king was dying. They threw down their weapons and asked for mercy from the English. Mowbray obliged, leaving a small force to watch the

The ruins of the hospital that was built on the spot where King Malcolm died of his wounds.

prisoners while he led the rest of his knights off to pursue the fleeing Scots and make sure they could not reform and return to the attack.

While Mowbray hunted the Scots up the north bank of the Aln, the wounded were being gathered together beside the small spring that bubbled to the surface near where the dying King Malcolm was lying. The king died later that day, but the spring soon acquired a reputation for having healing properties. Presumably many of the men who bathed their wounds in its waters recovered. For whatever reason the spring came to be highly regarded and some sixty years later St Leonard's Hospital was founded.

The death of Malcolm was a disaster for Scotland. The kingdom was plunged into civil war between Malcolm's brother

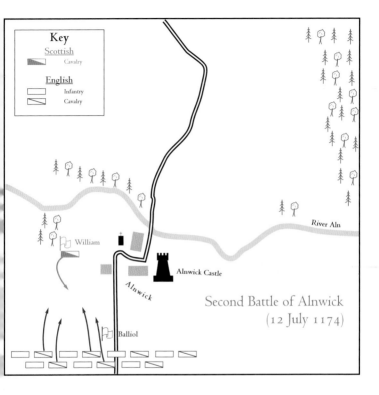

Key

Scottish

Cavalry

English

Infantry

Cavalry

William

Alnwick Castle

Alnwick

Balliol

River Aln

Second Battle of Alnwick
(12 July 1174)

Donald III and his sons Duncan, Edgar, Alexander and David.
Scotland was not to be peacefully reunited until 1124.

4. Just south of the ruins, turn right between a pair of stone
walls and on to a footpath that runs across the meadows
beside a wood to reach a lane beside a cottage. Turn left and
follow the lane over the Aln beside a weir.

5. Almost at once turn right along a footpath that runs uphill
to join a surfaced track. Turn left. On your right, behind some

The overgrown signpost that indicates where the walk turn right after recrossing the Aln to the south bank.

The slightly overgrown monument to the Second Battle of Alnwick lies behind some railings and can be easily missed.

railings, you will find the polished granite slab set on a sand-
stone plinth that serves as the monument to the second battle
fought at Alnwick, in 1174.

This second battle was, in fact, little more than a skirmish but
its political impact was immense. In that year England was in a
state of civil war as Henry II tried to put down his rebellious sons.
King William the Lion of Scotland decided to take advantage of
the confusion by invading England with the aim of annexing
Northumberland. He got as far as Alnwick without any serious
fighting, but like Malcolm before him was forced to try to capture
the castle before he could continue south.

After a few weeks the Scots began to run short of food, and the
Scottish troops were getting restive since they had come south to
plunder not to kick their heels in a siege. William decided to send
the bulk of his men off on pillaging raids across Northumberland
while he stayed at Alnwick to ensure the blockade of the castle
continued and no food supplies could be taken in.

The morning of 12 July dawned foggy and chill. King William
decided it was time to negotiate with the defenders of Alnwick,
and he rode forward to the castle gate to shout up his offered
terms. The English commander refused, so William turned around
to ride back to his camp. He had reached the spot marked by the
monument when the fog suddenly lifted. To William's horror the
entire hill to his left was filled with armed Englishmen.

The English may have been in the midst of a civil war, but the
northern barons had quickly put their differences to one side when
the Scots invaded. Led by Sir Ralf de Glanvil, Sir Odinel de
Umfraville and Sir Bernard Balliol, an army had marched out of
Newcastle some days earlier. They had been approaching Alnwick
cautiously through the fog as they knew the Scots outnumbered
them and did not know where the enemy was.

When the fog lifted to reveal the Scottish king with barely sixty men just yards in front of them, the English gave a cry of delight before surging forward. King William was nothing if not brave. He turned his horse towards the English, lowered his lance and charged. A few of his men followed him, but William was unhorsed almost at once and captured.

King William was taken south by the jubilant Balliol to be handed over to King Henry II. Henry had iron manacles put on the wrists and ankles of the Scottish king to emphasize his plight, then made William an offer. Henry wanted to concentrate on pacifying England, so he offered to let William go free if he first promised to allow English garrisons into the castles at Edinburgh, Stirling and Roxburgh. But the key demand was that William had to accept Henry as his feudal overlord. Desperate to return north, William agreed.

The deal struck by William and Henry was to have immense repercussions. The Kings of England had long claimed that they were vaguely superior to the Kings of Scotland. Since England was clearly a larger, wealthier and more powerful kingdom than the northern lands such a claim could be regarded as merely stating facts. But by accepting Henry as his feudal overlord William was putting the relationship on a clear legal basis. He would not be able to declare war, make treaties or even assign land to the Church without Henry's written approval.

Attempts by future kings of England to enforce this relationship on future kings of Scotland, and the Scottish monarchs' repeated efforts to maintain that the deal had been only for William and Henry, was to lead to many future wars and campaigns.

6. Continue along the track to return to Alnwick Castle.

5. CORBRIDGE
1312

Distance:	2½ miles.
Terrain:	This walk encounters no steep hills and is entirely over surfaced lanes and paths.
Public Transport:	The walk starts and finishes at Corbridge train station.
Parking:	On-street parking available in Corbridge and a small car park beside the bridge.
Refreshments:	Several pubs in Corbridge serving meals and shops selling snacks and soft drinks.

In 1312 England was in turmoil. Young King Edward II had been on the throne for just five years, but had already acquired a well-deserved reputation for incompetence. Matters were made worse by the fact that his long-term gay lover, Piers Gaveston, delighted in making cruel jokes about the leading noblemen and their families.

Finally the nobles had had enough. Led by the Earl of Lancaster they confronted the king, demanding reforms to the government, the sacking of corrupt officials and – above all – the exile of Gaveston. Edward agreed, but in February 1312 broke all his promises and recalled Gaveston from France. The magnates mustered their forces for war, while Edward and Gaveston sent messages abroad to hire mercenaries.

In Scotland Robert the Bruce, who claimed to be King of Scotland and in fact controlled most of the country, could scarcely believe his luck. English garrisons in Scotland marched south to join the preparations for civil war and border defences were abandoned. On 9 June the Earl of Lancaster murdered Gaveston, and the rival armies began to clash.

The view into Corbridge from the railway station. The walk runs along this road to reach the famous bridge.

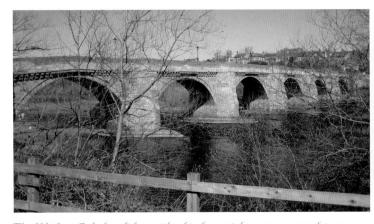

The old bridge at Corbridge, which was widened in the twentieth century to accommodate motor traffic. Until 1235 there was a ferry here. The present bridge was built in 1674 to replace the old medieval packhorse bridge. In 1771 it was the only bridge over the Tyne to survive the terrible floods that devastated the valley.

Taking advantage of the chaos, Bruce led a Scottish force on a fast-moving raid into England. On 12 August he crossed the border, raced to Haltwhistle, which was burnt down, and hurried back over the border. The Scots waited in some trepidation, but there was no English response at all. Nobles and king were too busy garrisoning fortresses and manoeuvring against each other to bother with the fate of Haltwhistle.

Emboldened, Bruce mustered a larger force for a more protracted attack into England. The army followed Redesdale down from the Cheviots, striking south with the aim of crossing the Tyne at Corbridge. If the king and nobles did not care about Scottish incursions the local Englishmen did. The question was, what would they do about it.

THE WALK

1. From Corbridge railway station head north along the B6529 to cross the old bridge into Corbridge itself. Turn left into Front Street, which becomes Watling Street as it bends right, then Stagshaw Road the B6529 as it heads north-east out of town. Halt at the roundabout where this B road meets the A69.

It was 8 September as Bruce and the Scottish army came down the road from the Cheviots. They came down what is now the B6529 and, as they approached Corbridge saw that the small town was defended. A small force of English militia was formed up outside the town gates and the walls behind them were manned.

At about this spot Bruce deployed his army from line of march into battle formations. It was soon clear that the advancing Scottish host greatly outnumbered the English force. After some desultory skirmishing, the English retreated inside the walls.

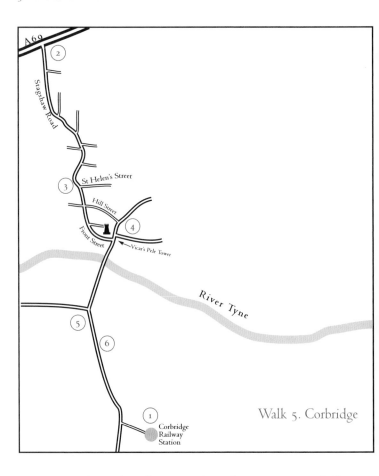

Walk 5. Corbridge

2. Return along Stagshaw Road to the junction with St Helen's Street.

The medieval town walls stood about here. They were not particularly impressive examples of military engineering. They had been designed to hold off border raiders and gangs of cattle

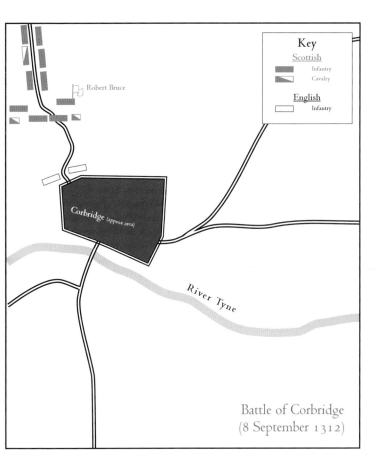

Battle of Corbridge
(8 September 1312)

thieves, not a full blown royal army. Both Bruce and the defenders must have known that a determined assault would over-
whelm the defences in a few hours. There was a pause while
Bruce reorganised his troops for the assault. Ladders were
brought forward and engineers set to decide on the weakest
point for the assault.

The majorty of men in Bruce's army were spearmen from the Lowlands. Their dress and equipment were specified in royal edicts. They had to carry a spear at least 10 feet long, a small round shield and wear a metal helmet. Sidearms were left to individual choice, but all men had to march with a thick cloak suitable for autumnal weather and a stout pair of shoes.

When the Scottish attacked, they swarmed up the ladders and over the walls to find that the English had gone. The defenders had only been trying to delay the Scots to allow the citizens to get away with their valuables and for the strategic bridge over the Tyne to be broken down behind them.

Undeterred by the abandoned town, the Scots soldiers moved through the houses methodically stealing anything that they could find and then setting fire to the town. By dusk the entire town was ablaze and a thick pall of smoke hung over the gutted wreckage of Corbridge.

3. Continue south along Watling Street, taking the next left into Hill Street. A short distance along this street on the right is the entrance to the churchyard beside which stands the vicar's pele tower.

△ Looking north from the most likely position of the English army. The Scots army came over the crest of the hill about a mile distant, then deployed across this road before advancing.

▷ Corbridge parish church. The tower was originally a Saxon belfry, but it was enlarged in early medieval times to be a fortified lookout, then turned back to serve as a belfry again once the border wars ended.

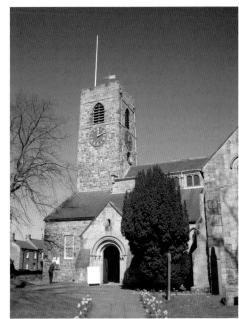

Left: The fortified pele tower in the centre of Corbridge. It was built as a refuge for the townsfolk by the Church after the sacking of the town and remained the official residence of the vicar until the eighteenth century. Right: The Market Cross which stood in the centre of the market place when the Scots attacked. It survived that onslaught, but was moved to a quiet corner when motor traffic made its original position inconvenient.

This three-storey fortified tower was built in 1318 using stones from the nearby ruined Roman fortress. It was designed to be able to hold out against even the most powerful army of Scots for several weeks, blocking access to the bridge to an invading army long enough for an English force to be mustered to come to the rescue. It fell into ruin after the joining of the two kingdoms in 1603, but was fully restored in the early twentieth century and now serves as a local museum.

The church is likewise worth a visit. The porch was not here in 1312, the inner doorway being then the outside door. The scorch marks that disfigure the stonework around the door were caused by a fire set by the Scots in 1312 as they looted the town.

4. At the end of Hill Street turn right into Princes Street and continue south over the bridge.

This bridge was built to replace the one destroyed in 1312, and has been repaired and widened more than once since.

5. Beyond the bridge pause to look across the field immediately south of the river.

This is where the army of Robert Bruce camped for almost two weeks after capturing and destroying the town. Raiding parties were sent out from here to destroy Hexham and to attack, with only limited success, Durham. The ravaging of the countryside was carried out with energy and efficiency.

Finally, around 20 September, a delegation of clergy from Durham arrived at the Scottish camp at Corbridge to ask what terms the Scottish king was willing to grant the gain peace. Bruce knew that the English were helpless and chose to be harsh. He demanded two thousand pounds in cash, plus the right to march freely through the bishopric of Durham any time he chose. The English were appalled, but there was little they could do except agree.

Robert Bruce called off his raiding parties and waited at Corbridge long enough to receive the first installments of silver coin. Then he went back the way he had come.

6. Continue south along the B6529 to return to Corbridge station.

The fighting at Corbridge had been minimal, but its effect was decisive. Edward II and his nobles patched up their differences in the cause of teaching Robert Bruce a lesson. Unfortunately,

Edward proved to be as incompetent at leading a campaign as at everything else. When he finally led a great army into Scotland in 1314 it was only to lead it to total disaster at the Battle of Bannockburn.

Robert Bruce became King of Scotland in name and in fact. Scotland became independent of England. Edward never recovered from the defeat and ended up being forced to abdicate by his nobles and then was murdered.

Two other battles were fought near Corbridge in 913 and 918. Both clashes came as Englishmen sought to defend the Tyne Valley from Viking raiders led by Ragnald of Norway. Other than the fact that Ragnald won both battles, no details have survived.

6. HALIDON HILL
1333

Distance:	2 miles.
Terrain:	This walk encounters no steep hills and is largely over surfaced lanes and tracks. However one section crosses open fields that can be slippery even in relatively dry weather.
Public Transport:	Berwick upon Tweed is well served by rail and bus routes, but there no public transport links from the town to the battlefield.
Parking:	A small car park beside the new battle monument, signposted off the A6105.
Refreshments:	No pubs or shops on the route of this walk, though plenty of both can be found in Berwick.

The town of Berwick upon Tweed as seen from the slopes of Halidon Hill. It was for possession of the town and castle that the battle was fought.

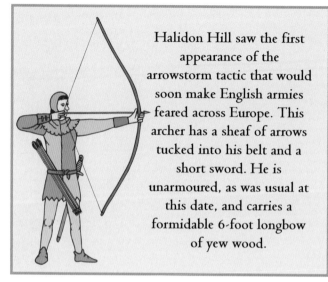

Halidon Hill saw the first appearance of the arrowstorm tactic that would soon make English armies feared across Europe. This archer has a sheaf of arrows tucked into his belt and a short sword. He is unarmoured, as was usual at this date, and carries a formidable 6-foot longbow of yew wood.

At the Battle of Bannockburn, fought near Stirling in 1314, Robert Bruce had defeated the army of English king Edward II and won for himself the crown of Scotland. However Bruce's death in 1329 reopened the long-running disputes between the Bruce and Balliol families over which had the better claim to the Scottish throne. While the victor of Bannockburn lived the Balliols accepted him as king, but Bruce died leaving only the five-year-old David as his heir. Edward Balliol stepped forward to claim the throne, sparking a Scottish civil war.

Events in Scotland were being watched carefully by King Edward III of England, who was keen to avenge his father's defeat. In 1332 Edward Balliol lost the civil war and fled to England. He asked Edward for military help, promising in return to honour the agreement made by William of Scotland after the Second Battle of Alnwick and acknowledge the King of England as his feudal superior. Edward insisted on one more concession, the return of Berwick upon Tweed to England, and then mustered an army to march north against Scotland.

Edward laid siege to Berwick, held for David Bruce by Sir Alexander Seton, on 12 April 1333. Realising that the defences were too strong to storm, Edward decided to starve the garrison out. A small watching force was left to blockade Berwick while Edward marched north to capture and burn Edinburgh. Much to Balliol's disappointment this did not cause the Scottish nobles to make peace. Edward, having no wish to be sucked into a long campaign inside Scotland, returned to Berwick, which he reached in June.

A large Scottish army led by Lord Archibald Douglas followed the English south from devastated Edinburgh. Rather than join battle, Douglas led his force around Berwick to lay siege to Bamburgh. The English queen was in residence at Bamburgh and Douglas hoped that the threat to his beloved wife would cause Edward to abandon the siege of Berwick, allowing the Scots to move in enough supplies and reinforcements to enable the town to hold out. The rather ungallant ruse failed. Edward stayed at Berwick.

Food in Berwick had now finally run out, so on 15 July Seton agreed to surrender Berwick on 20 July if he was not relieved by that date. Douglas now had no choice but to attack the main English army in open battle. He abandoned the siege of Bamburgh, crossed the Tweed and marched towards Berwick.

THE WALK

1. **In the small car park, find the modern battle monument.**

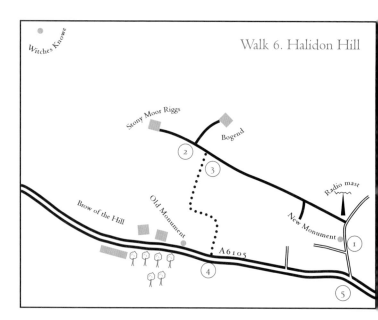

Walk 6. Halidon Hill

Witches Knowe

Stony Moor Riggs

Bogend

②

③

Radio mast

Brow of the Hill

Old Monument

New Monument

A6105

④

①

⑤

Over the years there has been a great deal of debate and disagreement among historians over the Battle of Halidon Hill. What happened is not really in doubt, but the lack of identifiable place names on these windswept hills has made it difficult to establish on the ground exactly where the events took place.

The battle monument contains a panoramic scene that is useful for identifying the various landmarks. It tells the story of the battle using what might be termed the 'southern approach' version of events. Since the monument was erected closer study of place names on old maps has indicated that an alternative 'northern approach' version might be the more accurate. This walks takes in both versions.

2. Leave the car park heading north along the narrow lane. At the summit of the hill turn left along a surfaced track beside a

Berwick Castle with the River Tweed beyond. The Scottish garrison in the castle had been under siege for weeks when the main Scottish army marched to their relief.

The monument and viewing platform on the south-eastern slopes of Halidon Hill. There is a small car park beside this monument where the walk begins and ends.

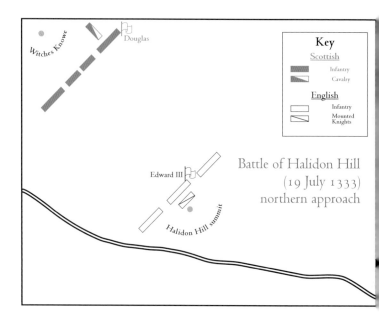

Key

Scottish

▰ Infantry

▰ Cavalry

English

▭ Infantry

▱ Mounted Knights

Witches Knowe

Douglas

Edward III

Halidon Hill summit

Battle of Halidon Hill (19 July 1333) northern approach

radio mast that leads to Stony Moor Riggs farm. Pause when you reach the side track to the right leading to the house named Bogend.

Following the 'northern approach' version, this spot was where the right wing of the English army was located. This right wing division was commanded by the Earl of Norfolk, aided by the Earl of Angus one of the few Scottish nobles supporting Balliol. The centre of the English army was commanded by Edward III himself, taking position just in front of the summit of Halidon Hill, visible to your left. The left wing, led by Balliol, was drawn up out of sight just beyond the hill crest. A force of some 200 knights was posted behind the centre.

At this date the primary weapon on the battlefield was the

After leaving the car park, the walk follows a lane for a few yards, then turns left into this gravel track that runs across the northern shoulder of the hill offering views to the North Sea to east and north.

mounted knight. A charge by a compact body of such men was the main attacking force available and was able to smash through infantry or cavalry with comparative ease. Most knights wore some forms of plate armour as well as head-to-toe mail. The arms and legs were frequently protected by sheets of iron, shaped to fit and buckled on with leather straps. The chest might also have been protected by strips of iron while the head was protected by a curved steel helmet with moveable visor. The 9 foot lance was the weapon of choice for the charge, though swords and axes were favoured for close combat.

During the previous few decades, however, the Scots had found an answer to the charge of armoured knights in the form of the shiltron. This was an infantry formation in which the men formed up in a dense oval or circular mass with spears 14 feet long being held out horizontally in all directions. The hedge of metal points dissuaded the horses of the knights from charging home and, once the horsemen were halted, the reach of the spears gave the Scots an advantage over the English knights with their shorter weapons.

Since their defeat at Bannockburn the English had been giving thought to how to defeat the shiltrons. Edward was advised by his seasoned northern commander Sir Gilbert Umfraville that the answer lay in archery. All medieval armies included archers, but they were generally mixed in with the infantry which dissipated the effect of their shooting. Moreover arrows were relatively expensive, so archers were inclined to shoot only when certain of hitting an enemy.

Edward decided to alter completely how archers were used. He recruited units made up exclusively of archers and paid for the arrows himself, so the men did not worry too much about wasted shots. The archers were then trained to shoot in massed volleys at targets pointed out to them by their archery commanders. The effect was to become known as the arrowstorm. Effectively several hundred arrows would descend from the sky on to a target in seconds. The archers were put on the flank of each division of the army.

Against the densely packed men of a shiltron, Edward hoped, the effect would be dramatic. Once the formation of the shiltron was lost, Edward planned to unleash a mounted charge by his 200 knights in reserve to drive the Scots from the field. Effectively he was hoping to use his archers to negate the shiltron and return battles to the good old days of knightly superiority.

From this point in the walk you should look north-west to see a second hilltop about a mile distant: Witches Knowe.

It was on Witches Knowe that the Scots formed up to attack. Douglas took command of the left wing of the Scottish army, with Robert Steward in the centre and the Earl of Moray on the right.

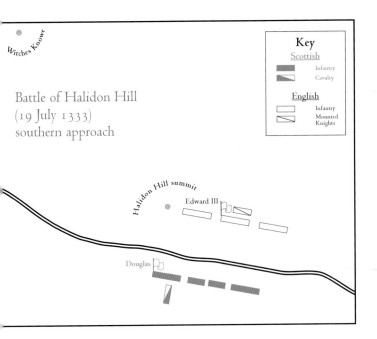

Battle of Halidon Hill
(19 July 1333)
southern approach

Witches Knowe

Halidon Hill summit

Edward III

Douglas

Key

Scottish

Infantry

Cavalry

English

Infantry

Mounted Knights

Each division was formed up into a shiltron, though the centre division may have formed two shiltrons. Behind his left wing Douglas had a force of mounted men with orders to make a dash for Berwick if the opportunity arose. If they could reach the town it would count as a relief and so Seton would not be honour bound to surrender.

Douglas had about 15,000 men to Edward's 10,000 and was confident of success. It was about 9am when he had his army in position and gave the order to advance. Moving slowly to preserve their dense formation, the Scots came down from Witches Knowe.

On the word of command, the English archers let fly their first volley. So well trained were these men that they could get the second arrow shot before the first reached its target. When the first

HALIDON HILL

9 JULY 1333

The old monument stands beside the A6105. There is no roadside path here so care should be taken when visiting it.

volley struck, the Scottish formations seemed to shiver. Lacking good quality armour, the Scottish infantry were horribly exposed to the arrows. Hundreds fell down dead or wounded. The second volley was as effective as the first, causing increased casualties.

Douglas gave the order to charge, realising that if his men did not close with the English quickly the arrows would kill them all. The pace quickened as the Scots broke into a jog, the formations becoming muddled and broken as they advanced. A third and fourth volley of arrows tore into Scottish ranks, but at last they were through the arrowstorm and could get to grips with the English infantry and dismounted knights.

By the time the Scots reached the English line their formation was so disrupted that the hoped-for impact was ruined. There were

The plethora of signs that adorn the wooden post beside the stile that carries the walk into a field from the gravel track.

some tense minutes of bitter hand-to-hand fighting, but the battle had effectively already been decided by the archers. The Scots failed to break the English line and began to fall back. As they disengaged, the Scots again became exposed to the archers, who let fly with deadly accuracy. The Scottish army broke up completely as the men turned to flee away from the deadly arrows as quickly as possible.

Seeing the enemy run, Edward unleashed his mounted knights. By this stage there was no real enemy army to attack, just a mass of fleeing, panicky men to cut down and harry. Scottish losses were very heavy, perhaps as many as half the men who had entered battle. English losses very light, probably under a thousand killed and wounded.

After leaving the car park, the walk follows a lane for a few yards, then turns left into this gravel track that runs across the northern shoulder of the hill offering views to the North Sea to east and north.

Berwick surrendered the next day and within weeks the Scots had accepted Balliol as their king. Young David Bruce was sent into exile in France. Edward III then made his mistake. Rather than being content with a friendly Scottish king, he demanded that all south-eastern Scotland be given to England. Balliol agreed, and so earned the enmity of his own people. Civil war broke out again and in 1341 David returned to be acclaimed King of Scotland.

3. Return back along the lane from Bogend to find a path turning right over the shoulder of Halidon Hill heading south. Follow this path along the side of a field, turn left along a hedge then turn right to enter a second field and drop down the hill to reach the main road, the A6105.

4. At the main road turn right to find the old battle monument, a massive boulder standing on the roadside. There is no footpath along this section of busy road, so care should be taken. Then return back along the A6105. Stop after about 300 yards.

According to the 'southern approach' version of events the Scots attacked from here, not from Witches Knowe. According to this scenario Edward had drawn his men up along the southern face of Halidon Hill, facing down on to this, the main road to Berwick. Douglas led his men off to the south of the road to form up before attacking. The subsequent train of events was then played out here, not to the north.

5. Continue along the A6105 and walk east to find the lane that runs uphill to the car park.

7. OTTERBURN
1388

Distance:	3½ miles.
Terrain:	This fairly long walk is mostly over open farmland, some ploughed and some under pasture, though there is a stretch alongside a main road. The going is muddy in all but the driest weather and includes a climb up and then down a steepish hill.
Public Transport:	Otterburn is served by the Munro's of Jedburgh route 131 from Newcastle.
Parking:	On-street parking in Otterburn village.
Refreshments:	A pub and a hotel serving meals and a shop selling snacks and soft drinks in Otterburn.

The Battle of Otterburn was one of the most famous events of the later Middle Ages. The almost impossibly chivalrous nature of the campaign appealed to the knights, minstrels and nobles of the time, ensuring that the tale was carried from one end of Christendom to the other, reports of it cropping up as far afield as Spain and Hungary. At least three ballads or poetic epics were composed about it and the tale remained a favourite entertainment for generations. As a result we know rather more about this battle than most medieval combats. Today the story is largely neglected since the political and military results of the battle were almost non-existent. It was, after all, fought over the ownership of a scrap of silk no more than three feet long.

In 1388 England was not a happy kingdom. The young King Richard II was proving himself to be a cruel, bad-tempered man, an untrustworthy ruler and habitual plotter. The great nobles neither liked nor trusted him, so they did not exert themselves much on

△ The Otterburn Tower Hotel, built on the site of and using some of the stones from the Otterburn Castle which featured in the premlinaries to the battle at Otterburn.

▷ The Otter Burn as it flows through the village, as seen from the bridge in the high street. At the time of the battle the stream was wider and more marshy than the modern, canalised stream to be seen today.

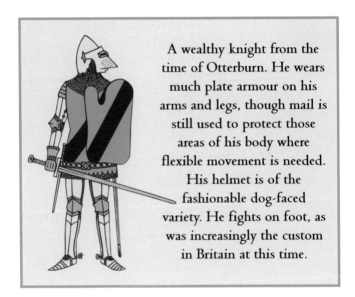

A wealthy knight from the time of Otterburn. He wears much plate armour on his arms and legs, though mail is still used to protect those areas of his body where flexible movement is needed. His helmet is of the fashionable dog-faced variety. He fights on foot, as was increasingly the custom in Britain at this time.

his behalf. The Hundred Years War against France was going badly and economic troubles had recently led to the Peasant's Revolt. The Scots, as ever, chose to take advantage of English troubles by raiding over the border.

King Robert II of Scotland had recently signed a treaty with France, and French military advisers were in Scotland to teach the northern warriors the skills that could defeat the English in battle. In July King Robert mustered a large army with which to invade and loot as much of northern England as possible. He chose not to march with the army himself, preferring to stay at home to keep an eye on his own troublesome nobles.

The invasion army was divided in two. The larger section was put under the command of the Earl of Moray and sent to attack Carlisle. It failed to capture the town or castle, but did immense damage as the soldiers fanned out over the countryside to loot and pillage. The smaller section, perhaps 8,000 strong, was allocated to James, Earl of Douglas, and sent to attack Durham.

In the later fourteenth century the Douglas family was at the height of its power and influence. Earl James was one of the richest men in Scotland, owning vast estates from which he could raise a substantial army of his own – and he had acquired a reputation as a chivalrous and skillful soldier. The chance to lead an army into England was just what he wanted.

Douglas led his men down Redesdale, along what is now the A68, crossed the Tyne and headed towards Durham. The city was stoutly defended, but when Douglas realised that no English army was nearby he ordered his army to break up into a number of smaller detachments to maximise the area that could be ransacked and pillaged. After several days, concerned that that the English might be mustering a large army to confront the raiders, Douglas gave the order to retreat.

The Scots recrossed the Tyne, but then Douglas heard that Sir Henry Percy was at Newcastle with only a small retinue. It was too good a chance to resist, so Douglas turned east towards the city. Sir Henry Percy was rather better known as Harry Hotspur because of his courage – almost recklessness – in battle. As the oldest son of the Earl of Northumberland, Hotspur was in many ways the English counterpart to Scottish Douglas. He was young, rich, famous and a renowned soldier. No wonder Douglas could not resist the chance to face Hotspur in battle.

When Douglas and the Scots arrived at Newcastle they found that the city was not so poorly defended as they had hoped. Hotspur was there, but he had with him more men than reported. Nevertheless Douglas decided to try his luck. He rode forward at the head of a small force of knights to inspect the defences at close quarters to see if any weaknesses could be spotted.

Hotspur saw the move and lived up to his reputation by

hurriedly donning his armour and ordering his knights to mount up and prepare for battle. As Douglas rode past the North Gate, the doors were suddenly thrown open and out charged Hotspur at the head of his men.

Hotspur made straight for Douglas. The clash between the two groups of knights was dramatic, but brief. The Scots fought bravely, but quickly fell back to the protection of their main army. The English jeered, but did not follow.

Only then was it realised that one of the Scottish knights had managed to grab hold of the Percy standard, tearing most of the silk banner from its staff. This was a great moral victory for the Scots and a humiliation for Hotspur. At this date each commander had a personal standard around which his men would rally and which was waved in particular patterns to convey orders to advance, retreat or change formation. They tended to be about one foot tall and three feet long and were composed of the owner's heraldic colours and embroidered with a personal badge and motto. A standard's loss in battle was a disgrace. To a proud man like Hotspur it was intolerable.

Galloping dangerously close to the massed Scottish ranks, Hotspur opened the visor of his helmet and shouted out that Douglas would never carry the standard over the border into Scotland. Then he rode back to Newcastle to make his arrangements.

Next morning, 18 August, Douglas and the Scots set out to return to Scotland. They stormed and captured Ponteland Castle that morning, then continued northwest towards Redesdale. Douglas kept them marching until dusk, when they reached Otterburn. This was more than thirty miles from Newcastle and only five miles from the border.

Next morning Douglas launched an assault on Otterburn Castle. The attack failed and by lunchtime the Scots were back at their camp. Douglas called a council of war. Most of his knights were in favour of getting over the Cheviots as quickly as possible, taking their vast store of loot with them. A few wanted to rest for the remainder of the day, then march home the next morning.

Douglas, however, had another plan. He believed that Harry Hotspur would try to make good his promise made outside Newcastle and would try to raise a force to catch the Scots. Believing that any such force would be small and hastily raised, Douglas wanted to stay at Otterburn to ambush it and inflict a second defeat on Hotspur. It was finally agreed that the Scots would remain at Otterburn, but only for a couple of days. If Hotspur did not show, the march to Scotland would continue.

Back at Newcastle, Hotspur was frantically trying to raise a force with which to chase Douglas. He had been in Newcastle because that was the designated mustering point for the army gathering to face the Scots, orders having gone out as soon as Douglas crossed the border. By late morning on 19 August, while Douglas was attacking Otterburn Castle, Hotspur was able to count 2,000 knights and 7,000 other soldiers gathered under the walls of Newcastle. It was enough. He gave the order to advance.

As the English marched towards Redesdale they were worried as to the location of the main Scottish army under Moray. They had no definite news of its position and Sir Ralph Ogle warned that Douglas might be luring them into a trap. The English were then met by a knight who had been sent out the previous evening on a fast horse to find the Scots. He reported that the Scots were halted in a camp a short distance beyond Otterburn castle, which was being attacked but was holding out. The was no sign of Moray, Douglas was on his own. On this information, Hotspur devised a plan and issued orders to his men.

Hotspur's plan was to divide his army in half. He would lead one half of his army straight up the road past Otterburn

Castle towards the Scots. Douglas, Hotspur calculated, would have his men drawn up astride the road and between the castle and his own camp. Hotspur would attack the Scottish army in this position.

Meanwhile, the second half of the army would be put under the command of the experienced local knight Sir Thomas Umfraville. These men would veer off the main road at Otterburn Castle and climb up the wooded hills behind. They would march through the woods for some distance, then turn left to come down the slope to take the left flank of the Scottish army in the rear. If the plan worked, the Scots would be surrounded and taken by surprise. Victory would be assured and Hotspur would get his banner back.

Back at Otterburn, Douglas was also laying his plans. They were remarkably similar to Hotspur's. Douglas planned to draw up half his army on a slight ridge that ran down from the wooded hills to the north down to the River Rede. The other half would remain out of sight behind the ridge and under the personal command of Douglas himself. When the English arrived, Douglas expected them to march straight along the road to attack his army, visible on the ridge. Once they were committed to this move, Douglas intended to march his own division up into the wooded hills, pass around the English flank, then storm down to attack it from the rear.

Douglas got his army organised, then settled down to wait.

THE WALK

1. In Otterburn find the Otterburn Tower Hotel. This is a Victorian construction that stands on the site of the medieval Otterburn Castle.

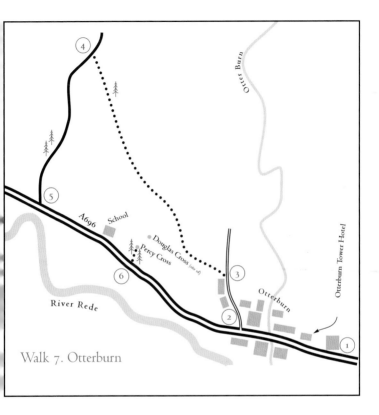

Walk 7. Otterburn

It was almost dusk by the time Hotspur and his men reached the castle. There was little sign of the Scots, for the men whom Douglas had posted on the ridge to the west had gone to eat their supper. Only a small group of scouts could be seen, one of whom quickly mounted his horse and galloped off out of sight. Hotspur hurriedly consulted the castle defenders in case the Scots had marched off hours before. Learning that they had not, Hotspur put his plan into action. Umfraville was sent off on his flank march, while Hotspur and his men advanced straight up the road.

2. Continue west through the village, crossing the Otter Burn until the end of the village is reached. Turn right up a lane signposted to Otterburn Hall, following in the footsteps of Umfraville.

If you look to the west at this point you will see a slight ridge on which stands a clump of trees beside the main road. This is the ridge where the Scots had planned to hold Hotspur's men while Douglas launched his flank attack. As Umfraville left the main road and pushed into the woods that then covered these hillsides the ridge was quickly filling up with armed Scotsmen. Hotspur moved forward slightly, but delayed his attack to give Umfraville time to march around to the rear of the Scots army.

3. Continue along the lane for about 200 yards, then turn left along a footpath that passes through a farmyard. This yard can be both squelchy and fragrant as the farm keeps a large herd of cattle. At the far end of the yard, pass through a gate (being careful to close it after you) and walk across an open field. At the far end of this field pass through a second gate, then cross a second large field. At the far end of this field the pasture ends and rougher moorland begins. Bear right towards a post visible on the skyline. On top of the hill the path meets a surfaced track.

This path runs roughly along the route taken by Umfraville, who was under orders to push deep in the woods than then grew here before turning left. When the path emerges on to the track it rejoins the route of Umfraville's march. By the time Umfraville got here it was night. Under the cover of the forest Umfraville and his men would have been in near total darkness. They were doing their best to head in the correct direction, but as they stumbled over tree roots and blundered about they seem to have lost their way somewhat.

△ The River Rede
immediately west of Otterburn.
The river with its steep,
overgrown banks formed an
obstacle that defined the
southern edge of the battlefield.

▷ The monument at Otterburn
stands in a small clump of trees.
The large upright stone was
originally a fireplace beam in
Otterburn Castle, which was
being demolished about the time
this monument was raised.

A view looking north from the monument. The Douglas Stone originally stood in the field to the right, marking the spot where the Earl of Douglas died.

Beyond the farmyard the walk crosses two fields of pasture along a tractor route before emerging on to open moorland. At the date of the battle all this area was heavily wooded.

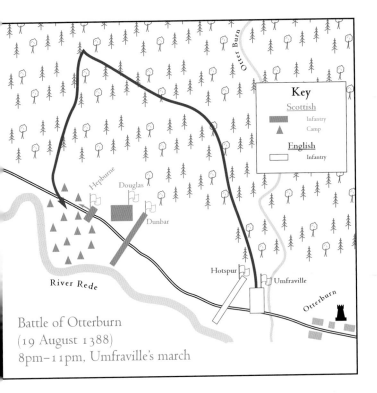

Battle of Otterburn
(19 August 1388)
8pm–11pm, Umfraville's march

Suddenly the disorientated Englishmen heard the sounds of battle. They were coming from behind them; they had gone too far through the woods. Umfraville seems to have reasoned that if he turned downhill he would eventually reach the road and river, enabling him to turn left and so find the rear of the Scots army. Accordingly he turned sharp left off his route.

4. **Turn left along the surfaced track. Pass two patches of woodland and pass through a gate, then continue down to the main road.**

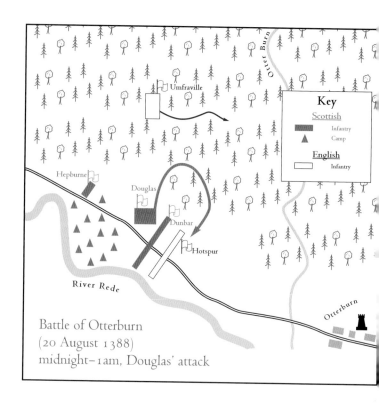

Battle of Otterburn
(20 August 1388)
midnight–1am, Douglas' attack

It was about here that Umfraville and his men blundered into
the Scottish camp. As they came out of the trees, the Englishmen
found themselves in bright moonlight for a full moon had risen
while they were in the forest. Douglas had left a formed body of
infantry in camp to protect the grooms and servants. In the confusion of a night attack on a camp of tents, wagons and temporary
huts the fighting soon got hopelessly confused. After some time,
Umfraville got control of the camp and began to push east towards
the sounds of fighting.

The English did not get far before they were met by a fresh body of Scots, apparently commanded by Sir Patrick Hepburne. Umfraville realised by this time that he had not only got lost on his way over the hill, but had lost any element of surprise that he might have had by virtue of the noisy fighting in the camp. He ordered a slow withdrawal back up the hill. After disengaging from Hepburne's men, Umfraville moved back through the forest towards Otterburn.

5. Turn left along the A696, passing the isolated village school, to reach the clump of trees on the low ridge. Enter the trees to find the battle monument, an upright stone set on a stepped stone plinth.

This stone marks the centre of the Scottish line on the ridge, and it was around here that the main battle was fought. The force holding the ridge was under the Earl of Dunbar. At first he had to withstand the full force of Hotspur's attack and the Scots were pushed back slightly. At one point a band of English knights, led by Sir Ralph Percy, younger brother of Hotspur, actually got through the Scottish line.

Seeing the danger, an impoverished Scottish knight named Sir John Maxwell left his place in the main line and led a small band of followers at Sir Ralph. Maxwell's onslaught tumbled Sir Ralph to the ground and, as he fell, the English knight had the great misfortune to receive a spear thrust in the buttocks. Unable to stand, Sir Ralph surrendered to Maxwell. The Scot first made sure that the Scottish line had been restored, then hauled Sir Ralph off to have his wounds bound up. The ransom he was able to get for this prestigious Englishman made Maxwell's fortune.

Dunbar had meanwhile stabilized his line and was holding the ridge while the battle raged in the moonlight. Suddenly a force of men erupted from the forest on the right flank of the English army. If Hotspur thought these men were those of Umfraville, he soon realised his mistake. A chanting song 'Douglas, For Douglas' burst from the throats of the newcomers. It was the Earl of Douglas and his flanking force.

Douglas had moved through the very edge of the forest, not pushing high up the slope as had Umfraville, and so had neither lost his way nor met Umfraville coming the other way.

Lifting high his great battleaxe, Douglas led his men forward in a great charge down into the flank of the English army. The English right flank was held by a Northumbrian knight named Sir Thomas Felton, then generally thought to be the handsomest man in northern England. This Felton tried to get his men to turn to face the new threat, but the Scots were on him before the difficult move could be completed. Fighting with prodigious personal strength, Felton momentarily held up Douglas's attack, but was cut down by a cousin of the Scottish king named Simon Gelendinning. Once Felton was down, Douglas and his men surged on.

As the English army disintegrated the battle degenerated into an unconnected series of small fights and savage close combats. In the confusion Hotspur was wrestled to the ground by Lord Montgomery, who managed to overcome the English nobleman and take him prisoner. All across the field Englishmen were either surrendering, fighting desperately or struggling to make their way back to the safety of Otterburn Castle.

Eventually the moon set and the cloak of complete darkness brought an end to the fighting. So complete was the dark that neither army was able to reform or get itself together in any meaningful way.

When the grey light of dawn crept up from the east it revealed a scene of confusion. A large number of Englishmen were huddled

The walk climbs over the moors by way of this strip of short grass through the heather and bracken.

around the walls of Otterburn Castle. Others were clustered together at intervals over the field. As soon as they could see, they bolted to join their fellows. Some minutes later Umfraville's men began to filter out of the forest and likewise made their way back to Otterburn Castle.

One English knight found himself in a dangerous position as dawn broke. Sir Matthew Redman had sought shelter in the edge of the forest and now saw that he could not hope to run to the castle before being spotted and caught by the Scots. As he wondered what to do, a riderless horse came wandering close to him. Redman managed to catch the horse and leapt into the saddle. No sooner had he done so than he was seen. A Scottish knight named Sir James Lindsay was mounted and gave chase.

Near the crest of the hill west of Otterburn the bridleway meets this narrow lane. The walk then turns left to follow in the footsteps of Lord Umfraville.

Redman spurred east down Redesdale, with Lindsay in hot pursuit. He managed to cover three miles before his horse stumbled and fell. Redman managed to draw his sword and get to his feet before Lindsay was upon him, but he was dazed from the fall and was soon beaten to the ground. Redman surrendered, but Lindsay had no real means of holding him captive. Instead he suggested that Redman give his promise to come to Edinburgh in three weeks time to present himself as a prisoner. In the mean time he was free to go home to put his affairs in order. Redman agreed, such arrangements being not uncommon in the days of chivalry.

The two men parted on good terms, with Redman riding off towards Newcastle and Lindsay heading back to Otterburn. Lindsay had not got far when he spotted a formed body of armed men sitting beside the main road. Taking them to be a party of Scots coming to join the hunt for fugitives, Lindsay rode up to the men. He was shocked to be suddenly pounced on and taken prisoner in his turn. The men were, in fact, the vanguard of a second English army advancing up Redesdale under the command of the Bishop of Durham.

Back at Otterburn the Scots were reforming themselves on the ridge where the battle had begun. Suddenly a shout from the hillside attracted attention. The cry had come from Sir William of North Berwick, who was lying wounded on the ground. A few Scotsmen approached to help the stricken man, then realised what it was Sir William had been shouting. The Earl of Douglas was dead, lying beside Sir William with a spear wound in his thigh and his head smashed in by an axe.

Mournfully the Scots lifted the body of their fallen leader and carried it back to camp. As was traditional in those days, a stone was found and set upright to mark the spot where Douglas had fallen.

The upright stone of the battle monument is not this original, but another stone put up in 1777 by the then head of the Percy family to commemorate the memory of his forebear Harry Hotspur. The Douglas Stone was then recorded to have stood about 200 feet north-east of where the Percy Stone was erected, but it has since vanished.

The Scots were too busy dealing with their wounded and their dead leader to bother with Otterburn Castle and the fugitives grouped around it. Grateful for the chance, the English moved off back down the road up which they had marched the previous day. After about a mile they met the force being led by the Bishop of Durham and passed on the news of defeat. Durham at once turned about and returned to Newcastle. There the captive Sir James Lindsay was met by his own captive, Sir Matthew Redman. The

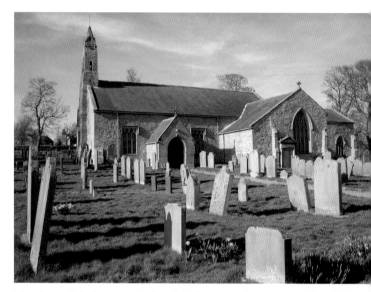

Near the crest of the hill west of Otterburn the bridleway meets this narrow lane. The walk then turns left to follow in the footsteps of Lord Umfraville.

two men agreed to exchange themselves, so both went home none the worse for their adventures.

The Scottish army, meanwhile, loaded its loot and wounded on to wagons and set off back up Redesdale to Scotland. They had won one of the most famous victories of the century, but came home in mourning for their dashing leader.

6. From the monument return to the main road. Turn left. Continue along the main road back to Otterburn village.

8. FULHOPE LAW
1400

Distance:	3¾ miles
Terrain:	This demanding walk goes over the high Cheviots, some of the wildest and most dramatic scenery in England. It is visually stunning, but the hills are steep and the paths rough and unsurfaced. It should be attempted only in the best of weather and even then only by those equipped with clothing and walking boots suitable for the high, bleak country.
Public Transport:	No public transport links to this battlefield.
Parking:	Car park at Buckham Bridge, where the walk starts and finishes.
Refreshments:	No refreshment facilities on this walk.

The year 1400 was a bad one for England, which naturally encouraged the Scots to raid over the border. This time, however, things were different from the usual scheme of things for the Scottish raiders were acting without permission of the Scottish king, but in the name of the King of England.

King Richard II of England had long been behaving as a ruthless and savage tyrant, and was becoming increasingly unpopular. In 1398 he banished without trial the popular Henry Bolingbroke, his own cousin and heir to the Duke of Lancaster. Early in 1399 the elderly Duke died. Richard at once announced that he was confiscating – again without any attempt at legal proceedings – all the lands, possessions and wealth of the Duke of Lancaster. Bolingbroke was to be left a penniless exile.

Naturally, Bolingbroke refused to accept this. On 4 July 1399 he landed on the Northumbrian coast with a small band of armed followers. He announced that he had come back to England to

▷ The signpost in the car park that indicates the start of the walk around Fulhope Law.

▽ The valley of the upper Coquet looking west from Fulhope. The high hills can be treacherous in winter, but in good weather the valley offers an easy droving route over the Cheviots with plenty of grazing.

demand a fair, legal hearing of the confiscation of his inheritance. Richard sent out orders ordering the immediate arrest of Bolingbroke, but nobody took any notice. Towns and castles threw open their gates, magnates rushed to join his cause and before long men were openly calling for Richard to be dethroned and Henry to be made king.

England stood poised for civil war. Then Harry Hotspur Percy and his father the Earl of Northumberland declared for Henry, supporting the call to make him king. The mere fact of Percy support decided many waverers to support Henry. But the Percies did even more. They mustered the armed men from their estates and marched south to back Henry.

The news that the Percies were marching south with all their men was greeted with joy and amazement in Scotland. At once men began to arm for a raid into England. However, King Robert III had problems of his own and did not want to provoke trouble with England. Robert's brother the Duke of Albany was engaged in an open and bloody feud with the king's son and heir, David, Duke of Rothesay. Another royal brother, Alexander, was busy trying to carve out an independent state in south-western Scotland and had earned the name of Wolf of Badenoch for his ruthless violence. Robert, or rather the Council then ruling in his name, refused to approve war against England.

In February 1400 the by now deposed Richard II died, almost certainly murdered on the orders of Bolingbroke, now Henry IV of England. The body was buried without being laid in state. Within weeks of the news reaching Edinburgh an Englishman arrived to announce that the body buried in Westminster was false and that he was the true King Richard II. He told a long and involved story of his alleged escape from Pontefract Castle, which few people took very seriously.

However the pretensions of the imposter provided a useful cover for those hungry to raid England. Claiming that they were acting for this exiled monarch, the reiver families of the border armed for war.

These reiver families were organised into close-knit clans, each based around a major family which could raise fighting men, tribute and money. They led a semi-independent existence at the best of times and given the chaos in Scotland at this time were free to do pretty much as they pleased. The usual course of events was for them to extort money from the nearby lowland farmers under threat of destructive raids. The money was collected in black pouches, hence the term blackmail. If a payment was missed a raid would be carried out. The autumn was the favoured raiding season as the long nights gave cover for operations, the bad weather had not yet closed in and the cattle to be stolen were fat and sleek from summer grazing.

The reiver families of the Grahams, Armstrongs, Elliots, Crosarys, Bells and Batesons put aside their private feuds, of which there were many, to organise a major raid in September of 1400. Reivers rode hardy mountain ponies and went to war in light armour, for their tactic was to move quickly, driving stolen cattle back home before the enemy could respond.

The massed reivers rode over the Cheviots, passing through Chatto before crossing the border by a high pass into the upper valley of the River Coquet. They then poured down from the wild hills to fan out across the lowlands around Rothbury.

But if the Percies had gone south, the Umfravilles had not. And this was Umfraville country. Despite Scottish hopes the system of watchers in the Cheviot valleys had been maintained. The man set to watch the Coquet saw the raiders and galloped off on his pony to warn the Umfravilles.

The nominal head of the family was young Thomas Umfraville, but he was only ten years old. Power over the Umfraville estates rested with his uncle Sir Robert Umfraville,

The farmstead of Fulhope looking east. The valley narrows suddenly and drastically just behind the house. It was here that the Scottish raiders sought to halt the pursuing English.

The track that runs down from the summit of Deels Hill to the hamlet of Makendon, out of sight beyond the shoulder of the hill.

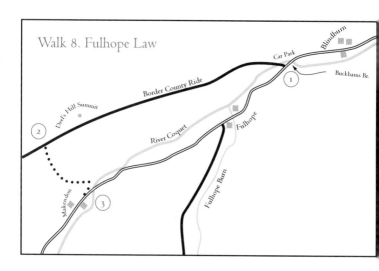

Walk 8. Fulhope Law

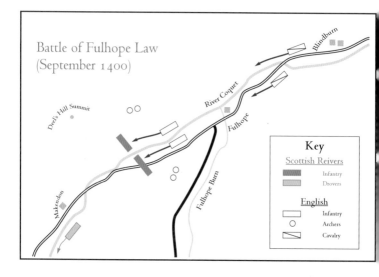

Battle of Fulhope Law
(September 1400)

Key

Scottish Reivers

▨ Infantry
▨ Drovers

English

▢ Infantry
○ Archers
▱ Cavalry

brother of the Sir Thomas Umfraville who had fought at Otterburn in 1388. Sir Robert was made of sterner stuff than his brother, and was not a man to make a mistake.

As soon as he heard that the reivers were on the move, Sir Robert sent out riders ordering everyone to make for the nearest fortified town or castle with as much as they could carry. He also summoned the men of Northumberland to war. Sir Robert knew that speed was to be the deciding factor in the campaign to follow. He commandeered every horse he could find. Whether it was a war horse, a riding horse, a plough horse or a half-trained mountain pony, Umfraville took it and put a man on its back. Then he rode hard for the Coquet Valley.

Umfraville reasoned that the reivers would go back to Scotland the way they had come. Rather than try to stop them as they were spread across the countryside raiding, Umfraville planned to ambush them as they headed home and crush them once and for all.

The reivers were no fools. They too moved fast and soon the campaign became little more than a race for the border. It was a close run thing, but it ended at Fulhope Law.

THE WALK

1. **Between Blindburn and Fulhope find the sole car park along this road where it crosses the River Coquet over a modern concrete bridge. The Border County Ride, a well signposted bridleway for horse riders, leaves the car park and strikes uphill towards the summit of Deel's Hill. Follow this track.**

The reivers got to this narrow valley first, but only just. They were moving slower than they would have liked due to the large numbers of cattle and horses that they had stolen. Herding these creatures slowed things down. As the reivers passed Fulhope they sighted the pursuing English coming up the valley behind them. Faced with the choice of abandoning their loot or fighting a rear-guard action, the Scots chose to fight.

2. Continue up the Border County Ride to the summit of Deel's Hill. This peak offers stunning views across the Cheviots and is the highest spot for miles around. Just beyond the summit a path leaves the Border County Ride to the left, plunging steeply downhill towards the road. Go down this path, but take care on the steep slope.

The Coquet Valley is at its narrowest here, and it was here that the reivers chose to fight. They formed up across the valley on foot, seeking to hold the English until nightfall while the cattle and horses were got away by the herders.

Coming up the valley, Umfraville also chose to dismount his men. The horses he had commandeered were not trained for battle, but had served their purpose in moving the troops faster than they could march on foot. Umfraville did not pause for long. He formed his men up in column, with archers on the flanks to shoot into the enemy formation. Then he attacked.

The archers inflicted casualties on the reivers, weakening their numbers and disrupting their formation. Then the English infantry charged home at the run. There were some minutes of savage fighting, then the reivers' line broke and the Scots fled west towards home.

Umfraville had foreseen the result and was prepared for it. He at once mounted his best men on to the fastest horses and set off in pursuit. The chase lasted until dusk and continued into Scotland. The reiver casualties were heavy, and Umfraville made a

The battlefield from the east. The area where the fighting took place has no public right of way through it, but it can be viewed from the route of the walk.

The battlefield seen from the road. The main fighting took place in the valley floor in the right middleground of this photo.

point of trying to capture alive any man who looked wealthy in the hope that he was a clan chief.

The ploy worked and Umfraville was able to lead back to Newcastle in chains several clan chiefs. Rather than execute these men, Umfraville chose to let them go – but only after imposing harsh conditions and fines. It was a clever move on Umfraville's part and it kept the central border region quiet for some years.

3. At the main road turn left. Continue along the road past the two houses of Fulhope to return to the start of the walk. If you do not fancy the stiff and demanding walk, you could walk (or drive) along the road to a layby on top of the hill west of Fulhope to gain views of the battlefield.

9. NESBIT
1402

Distance:	5½ miles.
Terrain:	This long but undemanding walk wanders over the flat lands beside the River Till, climbing only gently to reach the village of Doddington and hamlet of Nesbit. The paths are mostly unsurfaced and can be very muddy in wet weather.
Public Transport:	Glen Valley Tours bus route 464 runs from Berwick upon Tweed to Doddington.
Parking:	On-street parking in Doddington.
Refreshments:	No refreshment facilities on this walk, though both pubs serving meals and shops selling snacks and soft drinks can be found in nearby Wooler.

In 1400 George, Earl of Dunbar, fled the murderous intrigues of Scotland to seek safety in England. He was welcomed by the English King Henry IV who was keen for a Scot of standing who was willing to testify that the young Englishman then in Scotland and pretending to be the dead King Richard II of England was a fraud. This Dunbar did, and so was allowed to stay at Alnwick Castle under the careful watch, and lavish hospitality of the Earl of Northumberland.

Northumberland's watch was not as careful as it could have been. Whether with the active support of Northumberland, or on his own account, Dunbar raised a force of adventurous young men and raided over the border into the lands of his arch rival the Earl of Douglas. The raiders did not confine themselves to Douglas lands, but stole what they could from wherever they could find it before dashing back over the border to Northumberland.

The ruins of Doddington Bastle lie on private ground, but can be clearly seen from the road. The building is now roofless but in its day was one of the finer pele towers on the borders.

Understandably the local Scots failed to see much difference between being raided by a fugitive Scot and being raided by the English. They quickly mustered a force to raid into Northumberland and in early June they crossed the border. The force was relatively small, some 400 mounted men only thirty or so of whom were knights. But it was led by Sir Patrick Hepburn of Hailes, the son of the Sir Patrick Hepburn who had played such a significant role in the Battle of Otterburn.

Young Sir Patrick not only had a famous father, but was highly respected in his own right as a major landowner, brave soldier and honest man in an age when Scottish politics were dominated by treachery and murder. The raid may have been small, but it was prestigious so it attracted several other knights eager to make names for themselves, among them Sir John Haliburton of Dirletown, Sir Robert Lawder of Bass, Sir John Cockburn and Sir Thomas Haliburton.

Riding fast, the raiders achieved some success. Avoiding any castles or English garrisons they got as far south as Charlton before turning back. The Scots were now on the east side of the River Till, where the more prosperous villages and better raiding country was to be found. With Berwick and the crossing places of the lower Tweed in English hands, they had to cross the Till and strike west before returning to Scotland. The bridge at Etal was held by an English garrison, so they were probably heading for the ford north-west of Fenton as they clattered through Doddington on the morning of 22 June.

The English had not been idle, though Hepburn and his men had seen nothing of them. The Earl of Dunbar and his returned raiding force was in Berwick upon Tweed. Also in the town when news came in of the Scottish raid was Sir Henry Percy, the eldest son of the Earl of Northumberland who was better known as Hotspur for his bravery in battle. As usual, Hotspur was all for instant action and Dunbar agreed. The commander of the garrison at Berwick was not so certain and refused to allow the two noblemen to lead his garrison out. Quite properly he refused to allow the town and castle to be left vulnerable when the Scots were in warlike mood.

As a result Hotspur and Dunbar had only 200 men with them when they rode out of Berwick, heading south. As experienced border raiders themselves, Dunbar and Hotspur correctly guessed the route by which Hepburn and his men would make for home. Riding as hard as the Scots, the English likewise headed for the ford over the Till near Fenton.

It was the English who got there first.

THE WALK

1. In Doddington find the ruins of the bastle. They are partly hidden by trees a few yards south of the farm selling cheese and ice cream, identifiable by the comical life-size model cow outside.

This fortified manor house was built here in 1584 by the local landowner as a refuge for his tenants and their livestock when raiders came from Scotland. It was, therefore, not here in 1402. When peace came to northern England the bastle was no longer needed as a fortress, and soon proved to be rather uncomfortable as a home. It was converted to be a barn and storehouse and was not maintained as well as it should have been. During a powerful storm in 1896 the eastern wall collapsed, bringing the roof down with it and leaving the ruin that stands today.

2. From Doddington Bastle follow the lane that runs past the cheese farm north-west towards Nesbit and Fenton. After

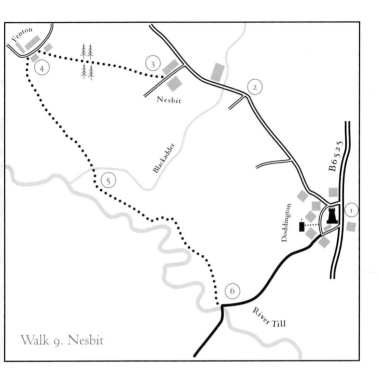

Walk 9. Nesbit

about three quarters of a mile the lane bends slightly left beside a track.

This was the route being taken by Hepburn and his men. It seems to have been at about this spot that they saw a group of horsemen coming out of Fenton and heading south across the meadows that lay beside the Till and Blackadder stream. Hepburn led his men off the road to ride west to intercept them.

As they rode across the meadows, the Scots will quickly have recognised the banners of Dunbar and Hotspur. They will also have realised that they outnumbered the English by some two to

△ The view across Nesbit Moor from Point 2 on the walk. The Cheviots dominate the background.

▷ From the little village of Nesbit the walk crosses several fields of sheep pasture. The ground underfoot is generally firm, but can be muddy in wet weather.

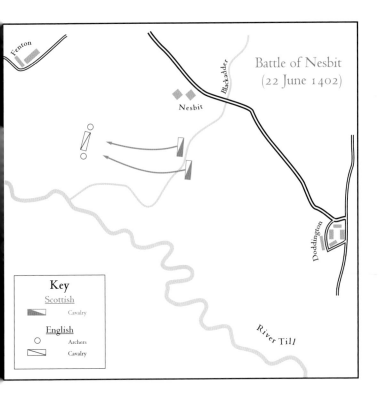

Battle of Nesbit
(22 June 1402)

Fenton

Blackadder

Nesbit

Doddington

River Till

Key

Scottish

Cavalry

English

○ Archers

▱ Cavalry

one. Presumably leaving the looted livestock and treasures behind with a small guard, Hepburn ordered an immediate attack.

3. Cross the small Blackadder stream, then turn left down a track to reach the hamlet of Nesbit. Just beyond the houses on the right turn right along a path that passes through a small grass field before striking over the meadows to enter a wood.

4. Beyond the wood continue straight on to enter Fenton. Turn left along a lane, then very soon left again to leave

Fenton along another path over the meadows, this time heading south-east.

This was the route being taken by Hotspur and Dunbar when they were spotted by Hepburn. In the late 1700s a local farmer found a broken sword in these meadows, which he sold to the local squire as a curiosity. Digging further the squire and his men found some ancient horseshoes and concluded that they had found the site of the battle.

It seems likely that they had, but unfortunately these amateur antiquarians did not keep a precise record of the location of their finds. They recorded only that the site was on the north side of the Blackadder, south-west of Nesbit House and close to the Till. The fight must therefore have taken place somewhere along the route of the modern footpath, but north of the Blackadder.

Among his men, Hotspur had some longbowmen. As the Scots charged, these men showered them with arrows, but the fusillade was not enough to break the Scots formation. The two bodies of horsemen clashed somewhere in these meadows. The English soon got the upperhand, perhaps because they were more heavily armoured than the raiders.

At one point Sir Patrick Hepburn went down to a savage sword blow. Seeing their leader fall dead, the Scots quickly lost heart. They began to flee, but caught east of the Till there was nowhere really for them to go. A few of the ordinary soldiers managed to get away and return to Scotland as fugitives but all the knights were killed or captured.

The Battle of Nesbit Moor was, in truth, little more than a skirmish. However, it was to have far-reaching effects that none who fought here could have foreseen. When the fugitives got back over the border to Scotland they spread the news that Sir Patrick Hepburn had been killed.

On reaching Fenton the walk turns left into this lane. It passes some farm buildings and a cottage on the left before turning off on to a footpath over Nesbit Moor.

Nesbit Moor looking south. The English were arrayed in the middle distance facing away from the camera.

The bridge at Point 6 of the walk. The walk picks up a surfaced lane here, bearing to the left away from the river and back to Doddington.

The death of the dashing young hero caused anger and fury across southern Scotland. Thousands of men began sharpening their weapons for war.

5. Continue along the path over the Blackadder stream, then follow the path over the meadows and alongside the River Till.

6. Where a bridge carries a track over the Till, join the track and follow it back to Doddington.

10. HOMILDON HILL
1402

Distance:	4 miles.
Terrain:	Climbing up and down two steep hills means this is not the easiest walk in the book, but the views are stunning and the surfaces are rarely broken or muddy.
Public Transport:	Glen Valley Tours bus route 464 runs from Berwick upon Tweed to Wooler.
Parking:	Very limited parking space at Humbleton and more extensive on-street parking in Wooler, half a mile to the east.
Refreshments:	No refreshment facilities on this walk, though both pubs serving meals and shops selling snacks and soft drinks can be found in nearby Wooler.

As the anger caused by the death of Sir Patrick Hepburn at the Battle of Nesbit swept through Scotland, encouraging news came from the south. King Henry IV of England had marched into Wales to put down a rebellion led by Owain Glyndwr, only to be met by torrential rain and ferocious storms which destroyed his tents and played havoc with his supply system. The English king was in trouble, the vague plans of the Scots to wreak revenge began to take definite form.

The leading advocate of an invasion of England was Archibald, Earl of Douglas. It was his lands that had been the target of Dunbar's raid earlier that year, and he who had the main motive in killing Dunbar or at least making his English hosts treat him as an unwelcome guest. When news of Henry's difficulties in Wales came through, Douglas turned to the Duke of Albany. Albany was the brother of the infirm King Robert III and effectively the ruler of the kingdom. The cunning Albany hesitated to declare formal war on

Homildon Hill as seen from Milfield, where the English army camped the night before the battle. Homildon is the central hill with the small peak pushing up above the skyline.

England, but gave Douglas permission to approach the Scottish magnates to ask them to join his invasion.

The Scottish army that mustered on the border late that August was a national army in all but name. Among those that answered the call of Douglas was Murdoch Stewart, Albany's eldest son, who brought with him most of the family's retainers. George Douglas, Earl of Angus, came with a powerful force. This George the Red, as he was generally known, was an illegitimate son of Douglas' father and the Countess of Angus who inherited his mother's titles and estates in the absence of a legitimate heir. A third earl, Thomas Dunbar, Earl of Moray, also came with his men.

It was not just the nobility who responded to a chance to raid England. The famous Fergus MacDouall came with a force from

Galloway. These Gallwegians were notoriously aggressive, but lacked modern arms. The Grahams came from the lowlands, so did their fellow lowlanders the Montgomeries, Erskines and Sinclairs. Even the Earl of Orkney turned up. As a further boost the group of French knights in Scotland to advise Albany on military matters volunteered to join the army. When he set off up the valley of the Ied Water to cross the border at Carter Bar, Douglas had about 12,000 men with him. It was the largest invasion of England that anyone could remember.

The vast Scottish force came pouring down Redesdale. Douglas paused to pay tribute to the memory of his honoured great uncle, the 2nd Earl of Douglas, who had died winning the Battle of Otterburn as the army marched over the battlefield. Unlike his fore-bear, Douglas found Otterburn Castle abandoned.

The English had suspected that the Scots would seek revenge for the death of Hepburn. The Earl of Northumberland had been excused duty on the Welsh campaign by Henry IV, as had all the northern barons and their men. Even the Sheriff of Lincoln had been sent back home when the scale of preparations north of the border became obvious. He was under orders to mass his men ready to march, but to await orders as to whether he was to go north or west depending on events.

Meanwhile the Earl of Northumberland was laying his plans well. He alerted all the northern counties to the possibility of inva-sion. The grain harvest was ordered to be gathered at the earliest possible moment and all stores of grain were to be taken to castles or walled towns for safe keeping. Fodder crops were likewise to be gathered in so that livestock could be taken off pasture and herded into safekeeping as soon as the Scots came over the border. The castles and towns were ordered to get their garrisons into fighting trim and to ensure that the walls were patrolled throughout the nights when the gates were locked as well as during the day.

Newcastle, taking no chances, put 100 men on night patrol duty.

Finally each lord and knight was given his place to muster when the Scots came. They were not to wait for orders, but as soon as they heard that the border had been crossed they were to raise their men and march. Some had the duty of holding strategic castles or towns, but most were ordered to gather at either Alnwick Castle or Dunstanburgh Castle, where the old earl had already begun gathering supplies and weapons.

If the Scots were making a major effort in the late summer of 1402, so were the English.

Douglas and his Scots came down into the Tyne Valley and spread out over the land to loot and plunder with enthusiasm. Finding no sign of an English army to oppose them, the Scots jubilantly concluded that the main fighting force of the north was with King Henry IV in Wales. Following age old custom they avoided strongly held castles and towns, but extorted money from those weakly held using the threat of instant storming and brutal massacre. Sweeping across the productive farmlands of Tyneside, the Scots succeeded in capturing sizeable numbers of cattle and sheep from villages that had not reacted quickly enough and had failed to get their livestock to safety.

Douglas advanced to the gates of Newcastle. Like his great uncle, Douglas paraded around the walls of the city as if looking for weak spots at which to launch an attack. None were to be found, so Douglas turned aside. Unlike the 2nd Earl in 1388, Douglas decided against returning back up Redesdale. He believed that the main fighting force of northern England was miles away to the south-west and that he had little to fear. There was nothing to stop the Scots looting and pillaging at will.

Douglas turned his army north, spreading out over the countryside from the North Sea to the inland hills. He was determined to scour England clean from Newcastle to Berwick. It was not until he was north of Rothbury that Douglas learned of an English army mustering at Alnwick. He pulled in the more far-flung looting parties so that they would not be caught by surprise by this reported force. Even so, Douglas remained confident that he could deal with any scratch force that the English had managed to pull together.

Receiving the news that Douglas was marching north to the east of the Cheviots, Northumberland led his army to Milfield. It was a strategic choice. Just to the east was the ford over the Till near Fenton while to the south was the River Glen. If the Scots came east of the Till, as Hepburn had done, the army could hold the ford and keep the Scots penned between the Till, the Tweed and the sea. If the Scots approached on the west of the Till the army could hurry the two miles south to block the ford over the Glen at Akeld. The Glen was not such a large river as the Till, but was still an obstacle to an army loaded down with loot.

As he came level with Alnwick, Douglas concentrated his army on the main road north along the foothills of the Cheviots. He splashed across the headwaters of the Till, not wanting to be caught on the wrong side of that river further downstream as had Hepburn earlier that year. Mounted scouts were sent out ahead of the army to keep an eye out for the English force.

It was at Wooler that the scouts came galloping back to Douglas. They brought the unwelcome news that an English force was gathered at Milfield, some six miles ahead. Even worse they reported that this was no mere scratch force of local levies. The English army was at least 8,000 strong and above it floated the banners of the northern nobles, including that of Harry Hotspur Percy.

For the first time Douglas realised that he faced a major battle. Even as he digested the news, the English army was on the march. Alerted by the arrival of the Scottish scouts, Northumberland was hurrying his men to Akeld to hold the ford there.

At this date, English tactics were based on the combination of the awesome firepower of massed ranks of longbowmen and the defensive might of dismounted knights and men at arms. The ideal situation was to draw up on a hill or behind a river where the enemy had only limited access to the English line. This likely spot for the attack would be held by a formation of armoured infantry drawn up six or eight ranks deep. These men would be flanked by large numbers of archers able to shoot thousands of arrows at the advancing enemy.

It must be assumed that Northumberland placed his men in the standard tactical formations. His knights and men at arms were dismounted and placed to block the ford over the Glen. The archers were put on their flanks, protected from direct attack by the river.

Continuing north through Wooler, Douglas will have come around the eastern end of Homildon Hill at what is now the village of Humbleton. Here he will have caught his first sight of the English army, drawn up to contest the crossing of the Glen.

This may have been Douglas' first independent command, but he was an experienced soldier and no fool. He knew that to attack the English in a prepared defensive position was simply asking for defeat. If he had any doubts on the matter, the French knights who had fought the English in France would have urged caution on him.

It was now late morning.

THE WALK

1. Follow the old main road, Burnhouse Road, from Humbleton village west to where it joins the A697. The section of the A697 around Wooler and Humbleton is a twentieth-century bypass, but from this point on it follows the line of the old road that was here in 1402.

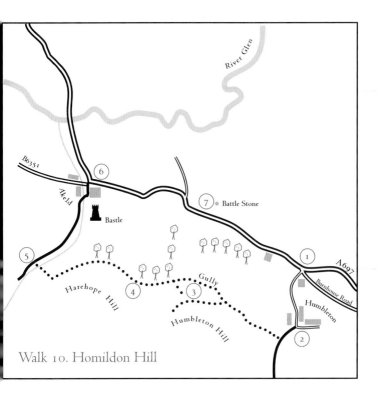

Walk 10. Homildon Hill

It was most likely at this spot that Douglas stood to view the distant English army and where he held a hurried council of war with his fellow nobles. Opinions differed, but the one thing on which everybody agreed was that no attack should be launched over the Glen.

The most likely explanation for what followed is that Douglas considered attempting to outflank the strong position taken up by Northumberland. At the Battle of Mauron, some years earlier, a force of 100 French knights had crushed over a thousand English archers after successfully launching a surprise charge from a flank.

The walk climbs up the southern flank of Homildon Hill up this lane from the hamlet of Humbleton. The Scots climbed the hill along this route as they prepared for battle.

Both Douglas and Northumberland would have known this. If Douglas could get a force of men across the Glen to threaten Northumberland's flank, the English might be forced to pull back to face the challenge, allowing the main Scots force to cross the ford at Akeld. Alternatively, Douglas may simply have been uncertain about the terrain and wanted to send out scouts to look for a safer route north for his army.

Whatever Douglas' intentions, he decided to put his army into a strong defensive position while scouts rode out to search the surrounding countryside. Looking round for a good spot, Douglas' eye fell on the towering heights of Homildon Hill (now Humbleton Hill) to his left.

△ The walk leaves the track by way of this stile to enter the open grazing that, then as now, covers the upper slopes of Homildon Hill.

▷ The walk diverges to the right here from the more trodden Hillfort Way. Although the walk follows a bridlepath, it is the footpath bearing left that is wider and better surfaced.

2. At the junction of the A697 and Burnhouse Road turn south up the narrow lane, signposted to Humbleton, that climbs steeply up to pass a phone box and then turns sharp left. At this corner leave the lane and follow a track that continues on up the hill. A short distance up this track a stile on the right gives access to a path that runs west across the face of Humbleton Hill. This path runs west for some 200 yards when it reaches the edge of a deep gully that cuts across the face of the hill. Here the path divides with a surfaced path bearing left and an unsurfaced bridleway bearing right. Follow the bridleway.

It was almost certainly here that Douglas arranged his amy in defensive array. The gully provided a convenient penning enclosure for the vast numbers of captured cattle, horses and livestock that the Scots were driving north with them. Here they could be corralled with ease by a few men. On its northern edge the gully has a pronounced lip on which the Scottish army could form up, facing downhill.

At this period the Scots generally preferred to avoid pitched battles when possible. However the victory at Otterburn in 1388 had encouraged them to believe that a determined attack could ensure victory, especially if delivered downhill and with superior numbers. What was not generally appreciated in Scottish noble circles was that at Otterburn, Douglas had achieved victory by launching his attack from the cover of a forest and thus achieved such surprise that the English had not been given time to deploy their archers in large numbers.

The majority of Douglas's army at Homildon would have been made up of lightly armoured infantry. Though many of these men rode ponies on campaign, they fought on foot. They came equipped with an iron helmet, usually without a face visor, and a wooden triangular shield. The main armour consisted of a long sleeved jack

The gully where the Scots almost certainly hid their baggage train and plunder before the battle began. The walk runs down to the tree then bears left alongside the stone wall.

The view downhill from the position of the left wing of the Scottish army. The English army was drawn up on the flat ground at the bottom of the slope behind the line of trees.

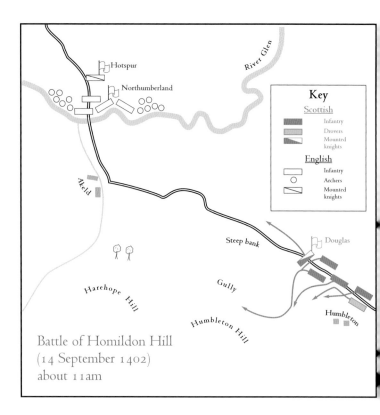

Battle of Homildon Hill
(14 September 1402)
about 11am

that reached down to the knees. This was usually consisted of linen
and wool up to fifteen layers thick quilted together and reinforced
by metal scales. Most men had mail gauntlets and some wore pieces
of plate armour on their chests or arms. For offensive purposes these
men carried a spear about 12 feet long and a sword for close work.
Thus equipped, the men could effectively ward off a cavalry charge
with their spears, and their armour was proof against glancing blows
from most weapons, though a determined sword or spear thrust
would break through.

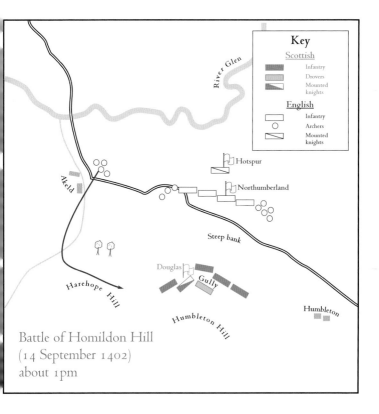

Battle of Homildon Hill
(14 September 1402)
about 1pm

One feature unique to Scotland was that all infantry answering a royal muster were expected to bring along a hunting horn. The purpose of this was so that at crucial moments the entire army could break out into a morale-boosting cacophony of sound that would drown out any enemy war cries, chants or songs. It was reported at one muster that the noise of the horns could be heard six miles away.

The Galwegians and some of the lowlanders would have been what was then known as ribaulds. Such men lacked the body

Looking towards Scotland from the position of the Scots army at the start of the battle. Akeld lies in the middle ground centre with the Scottish hills visible in the distance. The Scots so nearly made it home before they were caught.

Homildon Hill as seen from the position of the English archers on Harehope Hill. The Scots were drawn up on the saddle of fairly level ground in the centre of the photo facing to the left.

armour and spears, coming to war equipped with helmets, shields and either axes or swords. Some of these men were armed with bows, but they did not form up as masses of archers as did the English, but remained scattered among the rest of the infantry. Perhaps just as important, the Scots had to provide their own arrows. Costing as much as half a day's pay for a farm-hand, arrows were too expensive for most men to carry more than a dozen or so on campaign. The English, by contrast, had arrows paid for by their king and expected to have as many as forty-eight each.

Douglas seems to have arranged his army with the better armoured infantry forming the front line, with the Galwegians behind. His few mounted knights may have been on the left wing.

These knights, including Douglas himself, would by 1400 have been almost entirely encased in plate armour. Mail was used only to guard the less vulnerable places such as the backs of the thighs, or where free movement was essential, such as the neck. It was still the case that a co-ordinated mounted charge by a compact body of armoured knights was a devastating tactic. When used properly it could sweep an enemy army aside. It was, however, increasingly vulnerable to archery and could be driven off by well formed and tightly disciplined infantry.

In drawing up his army, Douglas seems to have been trying to avoid battle. He probably imagined that Northumberland would remain in his strong defensive position in the hope of luring the Scots into a suicidal attack. Douglas must have imagined that he had some hours, perhaps even a day or two, in which the two armies would both stand on the defensive. Plenty of time, he must have thought, to find a way around the English army.

It must have been with some surprise, therefore, that Douglas and the Scots saw the English begin to cross the ford and advance along the road towards Homildon Hill.

3. After exploring the gully and its lip, return to the path and head west to cross a fence by way of a stile.

This area was taken up by the left wing of the Scottish army. Looking down hill you will see a line of trees running across the hill. This hides a sheer drop or crag. It is only some 6 feet tall, but is large enough to disrupt the formation of a body of men, even more so mounted men. The trees were not there in 1402, but the drop was hidden from the Scots by a fold of ground.

From here Douglas watched the advancing English army. After marching along the road for a distance, the English swung off to the left to draw up in the fields on the far side of the highway. The Scots will have seen the English drawing up in their standard formation with dismounted knights and men-at-arms in the centre, with large bodies of archers on either flank. Douglas may have been disturbed, but was not yet worried. He was confident of the strength of his position.

But then about half of the English right wing archers detached themselves from the main army and headed back towards the ford at Akeld. If Douglas wondered where these men were going, he soon found out. In the early afternoon the archers reappeared over the shoulder of Harehope Hill, the hill that stands just to the west of Homildon Hill.

4. Continue along the path to the west as it drops downhill, crosses a boggy stream. Climb a stile towards a small wood. Passing the left side of the wood the path then climbs steeply up to the slopes of Harehope Hill. Pause about half way up the slope.

This was where the English archers drew up. Looking back over the stream and its ravine you get a good view of the Scottish

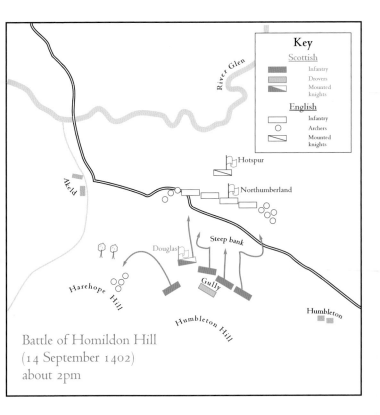

Battle of Homildon Hill
(14 September 1402)
about 2pm

position that you have just left. The Scots were about 200 yards distant, getting on for the longest range over which a longbow could be shot with any degree of accuracy. But with the Scots infantry massed together in a defensive schiltron formation the English could hardly miss.

Casualties among the Scots began to mount alarmingly and quickly. The unarmoured Galwegians and ribaulds suffered most from the arrowstorm. Those infantry wearing helmets and quilted jerkins did have at least some protection from the long range shoot-

The lower slopes of Homildon Hill. The charge by the Scottish army came down from the hill to the right to attack the English army, drawn up on the level ground at the foot of the hill to the left.

ing, but even they began to receive wounds and to be killed. Douglas seems to have been paralysed by the sudden shock of seeing his great plans for glory and victory suddenly turning to defeat in front of his eyes. His aides begged him for orders, but he simply stood staring in bemusement at the English.

In the front ranks of the small contingent of mounted knights with the Scottish army were Sir John Swinton and Sir Adam Gordon. The Swintons and Gordons were in 1402 in the midst of an ugly and brutal feud, but the two knights respected each other's skills in battle. As the English arrows continued to rain down around them, the two knights turned to each other to express their disgust at the lack of orders from Douglas.

Suddenly the English archers on Harehope Hill saw a ripple of movement among the knights. Something was at last about to happen.

5. Continue along the path as it goes around the shoulder of Harehope Hill to pass a second wood and emerges on to a surfaced track beside a small stream tumbling down from the heights above. This was the route taken up the hill by the English archers and, as can be seen by glancing back towards Humbleton Hill, was out of sight of the Scottish forces. At the track turn right down the hill.

At the base of the hill is the village of Akeld. To your right as you enter the village is what appears to be a stone barn, but is in fact Akeld Bastle. This is just one of several bastles, or fortified block-houses, scattered across England about a day's march south of the border. This one was erected in about 1520, so it was not here on the day of battle. Most of the time such bastles stood empty, but when danger from Scotland threatened they were given small garrisons – that of Akeld was twenty men. Their duty was to keep watch on the roads for signs of the Scots. Although they were not intended to withstand a siege by a major army, with walls over 6 feet thick these bastle could hold out against smaller raiding parties.

Akeld Bastle is now used as a cattle barn, with a nineteenth century hayloft having been added above. It is not open to the public, but can be seen from the track quite clearly. The old arrow slits and gunports remain.

6. In Akeld turn right to walk along the main A697. There is no surfaced footpath along this stretch, but broad grass verges provide easy walking. After about three quarters of a mile a lane enters the main road from the left.

This junction marks the approximate position of the right wing of the main English army. It was drawn up facing south towards the Scots on the slopes of Homildon Hill. The left wing of the army was some 700 yards further along the main road. If you follow the road, you will cross a small stream and then see a standing stone in a field to your left. This Battle Stone is generally held to mark the centre of the English army, though it may mark a mass grave or perhaps the spot where the Earl of Northumberland planted his standard during the battle.

From here the English archers and knights saw the same ripple of movement among the Scottish knights as had the archers up on Harehope Hill. Suddenly a section of the Scottish cavalry launched itself down the hill. These were the retainers of Sir John Swinton and Sir Adam Gordon, who had finally given up on Douglas and decided to act on their own account. There were barely a hundred of them, but they came storming down the slopes towards the waiting English.

Drawn up as they were on flat, open ground with no natural obstacles to guard their flanks, the English were far from being in their ideal defensive position. However the land between them and the Scots was open, providing an ideal field of fire to the archers. As Swinton and Gordon came thundering down the slope, they were met by a deadly hail of arrows. The armoured men did not suffer unduly, but the horses suffered badly. As each horse fell it took its rider with it. Soon the small charge was reduced to a rabble of dismounted, dazed men and riders struggling to control wounded horses.

The action of the small band of Scots at last shook Douglas out of his daze. He led the main force of mounted knights down the hill towards the English to support Swinton and Gordon, ordering the schiltron of spear-armed infantry to follow him as fast as possible. A smaller force was to head west towards Akeld to try to outflank the archers on Harehope Hill.

Douglas's mounted charge fared no better than had that of Swinton and Gordon. Meanwhile the advancing schiltron had

The bastle at Akeld. Built long after the battle this was a key feature in the English chain of border defences that prevented any repetition of the earlier large scale raids, such as that which occurred at Homildon Hill.

encountered the sudden, steep bank near the foot of the hill. A man alone could have simply jumped down, but a densely packed formation of several thousand men could not. Some tried to flow around the sides of the obstacle, others scrambled down it. The orderly ranks of the Scottish infantry became hopelessly muddled.

All this time the fearsome arrowstorm of the English was continuing to rain down from the skies, inflicting wounds and sudden death with alarming speed. Douglas himself fell from his horse when an arrow punched through the visor of his helmet to inflict a face wound that cost him an eye and hideously scarred him for life. Disordered by the bank, losing men fast to the arrows and now with their leader down, the Scots army suddenly disintegrated.

Turning west to pour through the gap between the hill and the right flank of the English army, the Scottish force collapsed within minutes into a fleeing mob. Weapons and arms were thrown aside as the Scots realised that their only chance to escape the deadly hail of arrows was to run.

This was the moment for which Sir Henry 'Hotspur' Percy, son and heir of Northumberland, had been waiting. He commanded the small force of mounted knights positioned behind the archers and dismounted knights of the main English force. Seeing the Scots run, he raised his banner and set off in pursuit. Northumberland wasted little time getting a force of archers mounted on to their ponies and sent off to support his son.

Whenever a group of Scots looked as if they might rally, the archers dismounted to shoot them down from a distance. When they ran, the Scots found themselves chased by Hotspur's cavalry with their lances and swords. The slaughter was horrible. Even hardened warriors were aghast at the killing being done that day. The chase, and the carnage, continued until nightfall.

Next day the English began the task of stripping the dead of valuables, and of any weapons and armour that could be salvaged. Then the dead knights were identified by their coats of arms and a message prepared announcing the casualty list. The English gave up counting the numbers of non-noble dead as there were so many. It is thought that as many as 3,000 Scots died on Homildon Hill itself and perhaps as many more again between the hill and the Tweed. Certainly the governor of Berwick later reported that his men had pulled 500 Scottish bodies out of the river, and that many more had been lost in the waters.

In all perhaps 8,000 of Douglas's army of 12,000 died that day. Northumberland and his army lost only five men. The great damage had been inflicted by the archers from a distance, the Scots army never getting to hand-to-hand combat with the English.

The Battle Stone which marks the likely site of the English right wing during the battle.

As ever noble prisoners were highly sought after because of the ransoms that could be gained for them. During the chase, the English went to great lengths to capture rich men alive, while any noble who was wounded could be assured of good medical treatment. The prisoners included not only the wounded Douglas himself, but also Murdoch Stewart, the earls of Moray, Angus and Orkney; the barons of Montgomery, Erskine, Seton and Abernethy; Sir Robert Logan, Sir William Graham, Sir Adam Forester, Sir David Fleming and the French nobleman Pierre des Essarts.

7. From the Battle Stone, continue along the A6976 to return to the start of the walk at the junction with Burnhouse Road.

This is the end of the walk, but the route of the Scottish retreat can be followed by car. Head north along the A697 as far as Crookham. Up to this point the River Till runs close to the high hills to the west, restricting the directions the Scots could take and making them easy to catch. Beyond Crookham the line of hills pulls back to the west, while the Till turns north past Etal to the Tweed. Here the stream of fugitives spread out over the land, dispersing in panic and making the job of Hotspur and his men more difficult.

Continue along the A697 to Coldstream. The bridge here was the magnet that drew the majority of the Scots, though many of the more lightly armoured men plunged into the Tweed and swam across. Just before Coldstream you could turn left along the B6350 to Kelso, where a second bridge offered hopes of escape and to which many Scots fled.

II. HEDGELEY MOOR
1464

Distance:	3 miles.
Terrain:	There are no steep hills on this walk, and some of it is over surfaced lanes. However one long stretch goes across open fields that can be muddy after rain.
Public Transport:	Travelsure bus 473 runs from Alnwick to Wooperton, stopping at Percy's Leap.
Parking:	Very limited parking space in a layby at Percy's Leap, which is signposted on the A697 just south of Wooperton.
Refreshments:	No refreshment facilities on this walk, though both pubs serving meals and shops selling snacks and soft drinks can be found in Wooler, a short drive to the north.

The dynastic tangles, internecine feuding and constantly changing allegiances of the Wars of the Roses are notoriously complex. The key issues at stake were, however, clear. When Henry IV had deposed and murdered King Richard II he had done so despite the fact that Edmund Mortimer, Earl of March, actually had a better claim to the throne. However Mortimer was only a child and England needed a capable, adult ruler.

Henry IV and his son Henry V were both competent and successful rulers who ran government efficiently, ensured justice was given fairly, kept the barons in check and defeated France at war. Mortimer and his children wisely kept their heads down and everyone was content. However, King Henry VI was a very different monarch. Good-natured, religious and generous the new king was a pleasant enough man, but a weak and indecisive king. By 1453 it could no longer be hidden that the king was also simple-minded and subject to spasms of insanity.

Percy's Lancastrians were drawn up in this field, facing to the left with the small stream protecting their front. The men of Lords Roos and Hungerford were behind the camera.

Percy's Cross stands in the back garden of a cottage, surrounded by iron railings. It can be approached by way of a public footpath off the main road.

The rule of England had suffered greatly during this Henry's reign. His grasping and corrupt queen, Margaret of Anjou, packed government with like-minded cronies who milked government of its funds and sold offices to the highest bidder. Inevitably the government got into financial difficulties and raised harsh new taxes. Justice ceased to be impartial and the war with France went badly. When King Henry lapsed into madness in 1453 the Council and Parliament called upon Richard Duke of York to take over the government. York did so with energy and competence. Within a few months he had the royal finances back in credit, had sacked corrupt officials and judges and generally got things in order.

On 28 December 1454 King Henry suddenly got up from the chair in which he had been sitting for eighteen months. So far as he was aware he had sat down about five minutes earlier, and was now back to his old self. York resigned as regent and before long Queen Margaret was back to her old tricks.

There were some bad tempered brawls between the supporters of York and Margaret, the latter being known as Lancastrians since Henry was descended from the Duke of Lancaster. In 1460 Margaret had York murdered and open warfare erupted.

Most of the fighting took place far to the south of Northumberland and by Christmas 1463 it seemed that the matter had been decided. York's son Edward was now on the throne as Edward IV, while the Lancastrians were reduced to holding only a few castles. In Northumberland these included Alnwick, Bamburgh, Hexham, Bywell, Dunstanburgh and Langley – some of the greatest fortresses of the kingdom. Henry VI himself was at Bywell. Queen Margaret, meanwhile, was on a whirlwind tour to drum up support abroad. King James III of Scotland was backing the Lancastrians, as was King Louis XI of France and Margaret was moving on to secure support and backing elsewhere.

Edward was not idle, however. He had been exchanging messages with King James and in March it was agreed that ambassadors would go north to Edinburgh to negotiate a deal. Edward was desperate to stop the flow of supplies and men reaching the Lancastrians in their northern castles, while James had his eyes on English silver.

Nobody was in any doubt that a deal would be reached. When they heard the news, the Lancastrians moved swiftly to sabotage the deal before it could be agreed.

Edward's ambassadors were travelling north with an escort of eighty knights and men-at-arms plus a few hundred archers led by Lord Montagu, younger brother of the mighty Earl of Warwick. Early in April the ambassadors reached Newcastle. After stopping for a few days they set off north and only narrowly escaped riding into an ambush laid by the Lancastrian Duke of Somerset a few miles north of the city. Balked of his prey, Somerset decided to concentrate on guarding Henry VI instead and returned to Hexham.

Another Lancastrian, Sir Ralph Percy, decided to make another attempt on Montagu and the ambassadors. Sir Ralph was the second son of the Earl of Northumberland and a much respected figure in the north. Northumberland and the Percies had supported Henry VI against York, the 3rd Earl being killed in battle in 1461 and Henry, 4th Earl, being at this date held in comfortable imprisonment in London while he and Edward negotiated.

Sir Ralph's activities on behalf of the Lancastrians were not backed by his father or brothers who preferred to come to a deal with Edward. Nevertheless his own popularity and the magic of the Percy name ensured that Sir Ralph could raise men in the north. By late April he had about 2,000 men gathered at Wooler. There he was joined by Lord Roos and Lord Hungerford, who each brought just over a thousand men.

An armoured cavalryman of the Wars of the Roses.
Men such as this were used to scout ahead of an
army and provide flank cover in battle. At
Hedgeley Moor the Yorkists pursued and defeated
Lancastrians led by Roos and Hungerford with
such men.

Percy now moved south to Wooperton. He knew that Montagu and the ambassadors would avoid the Lancastrian fortress of Alnwick that guarded the main road north to Scotland. He guessed correctly that they would head north along what is now the A697, skirting the eastern edge of the Cheviots. At Wooperton those hills came very close to the River Breamish creating a narrow gap where Percy felt confident he could block the road. He seems to have camped his army just north of a narrow stream, perhaps intending to use the stream as an obstacle in front of his army for he intended to fight a defensive battle even though his forces greatly outnumbered those of Montagu.

What Percy did not realise was that after escaping the abortive ambush by Somerset, Montagu had paused at Newcastle to gather reinforcements. The cause of York was popular among the towns and cities of Yorkshire, so before long Montagu had some 4,000 men under his command. He then headed north and on 25 April came in sight of Percy's Lancastrians.

THE WALK

1. On the A697 find the layby next to the stones known as Percy's Leap. There is a display sign beside the layby that gives some details of the battle. From the layby walk south alongside the main road to find where it crosses a small stream beside a belt of woodland to the left of the road. A row of cottage stands on the left south of the stream.

There is some disagreement over exactly where Percy positioned his men to face those of Montagu. Contemporaries recorded the place of battle as Hedgeley Moor, a rather vague term for the open land south of Wooperton. Some claim that Percy put his men on

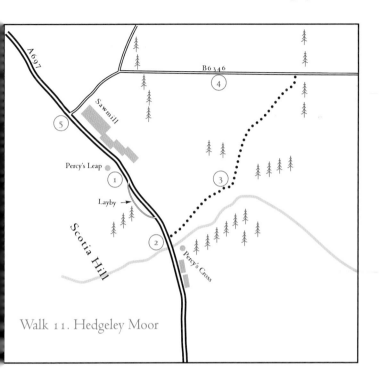

Walk 11. Hedgeley Moor

the slopes of Scotia Hill, west of the main road, others that he had them lined up at Wooperton itself.

However, about ten years after the battle the 4th Earl of Northumberland, Percy's brother, erected a tall stone cross to commemorate the battle, carving it with the family arms and the heraldic devices of others who fought here. This cross stands beside the small stream. It was usual for upright stones or crosses to be erected to mark the place where a famous man fell or where he had his standard planted. It must be assumed that the 4th Earl would have taken the trouble to put the monument in the right place, so it is most likely that Percy and the Lancastrians were drawn up on the north bank of this stream. The monument is in the garden of a cottage, but can be accessed by way of a gate.

The stream is today merely a narrow trickle of water. Back in 1464 it would have been little larger, but the moor had not then been drained into productive farmland so the stream would have been bordered by belts of marshy ground that would have slowed the assault of heavily armoured men.

Percy's Cross, as the monument is known, stands about 50 yards from the road surrounded by iron railings. The carvings have become rather weathered by centuries of standing open to the elements, but the key features can be made out.

Percy put himself and his own supporters astride the road with his right flank resting on the lower slopes of Scotia Hill. To his left was Lord Roos and beyond him Lord Hungerford.

2. Just before the cottages a small gate gives access into a wood. A path leads through the wood to reach Percy's Cross. Return back to the main road and head north to where a signpost indicates a stile that should be crossed. The footpath does not begin well, passing through what appears to be an overgrown rubbish tip, but after about 100 yards it emerges into scenic open farmland.

This is where the left flank of Hungerford's force rested. His force may have been drawn back slightly from the stream to avoid boggy ground. Today a small wood blocks the view south, but in 1464 this was open moorland and there was nothing to stop Hungerford's men from getting a clear view of the Yorkist column as it approached.

As Montagu's men came marching up the old Roman road from the south, the Lancastrians got their first view of what they faced. Instead of the eighty knights and a few hundred archers that they

The walk passes through this rather uninviting wasteground as it leaves the A697. This stretch is barely 100 yards long before the walk emerges into open farmland.

Beyond the wasteground the walk crosses this pasture field, then the arable land beyond to emerge on to a surfaced lane beside the small wood visible in the centre distance.

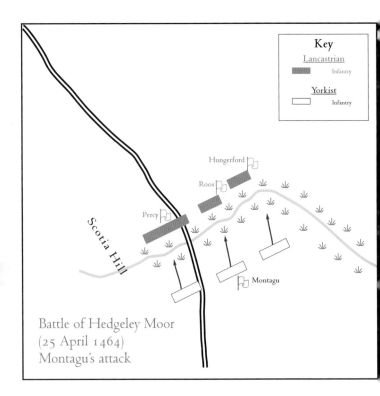

Battle of Hedgeley Moor
(25 April 1464)
Montagu's attack

had been expecting they saw some 4,000 men approaching. It was a nasty shock.

When about 400 yards south of the Lancastrian position, Montagu halted his column. He spread his men out into a battle formation that took the form of a line facing north and about the same width as that of the Lancastrians. With trumpets blaring and banners waving, the Yorkists then advanced to the attack.

As was customary at this date, the Yorkists halted some 150 yards from the enemy so that the archers of the opposing armies could let fly their deadly missiles. For several minutes the arrows flew back and forth, then Montagu waved his standard to give the signal for the dismounted knights and men-at-arms to advance over the stream.

It was too much for Hungerford's men. Expecting merely to block a small detachment, they had found themselves engaged in a pitched battle with a determined enemy. They began to edge back, then took to their heels and fled. Almost equally nervous were the men of Lord Roos. When Hungerford's men bolted, these men likewise began to fall back, though they seem to have kept rather better order.

3. Continue along the footpath. it crosses one open field, then bears left alongside a fence to reach a small copse before striking off across the middle of an arable field, through a gate and then uphill over a second large field. It finally emerges on to a surfaced road beside a small wood. Turn left along the lane and continue about 500 yards until you are roughly half way towards a group of trees visible on both sides of the road.

It was somewhere here that Roos's men finally gave way to join Hungerford's men in desperate flight north. Percy's men were still fighting well, having fallen back only a slight distance to keep in touch with their fellows. It was now that Montagu showed his skills as a battlefield commander. Instead of loosing his men to pursue the fleeing Lancastrians, he shouted orders to keep them in formation. Not all of his men obeyed, but the majority did. Montagu was thus able to swing them around to attack Percy's division in its flank and rear, pushing the Lancastrians back against the slopes of Scotia Hill.

4. Continue along the lane to pass through the trees, ignoring a turning to the right. The lane emerges back on to the A697 beside a sawmill. Turn left.

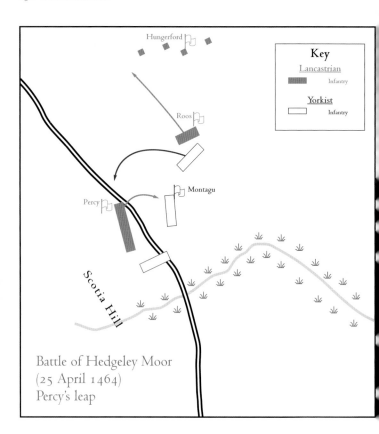

Battle of Hedgeley Moor
(25 April 1464)
Percy's leap

5. Continue south along the A697 to return to the layby and the start of the walk. The stones of Percy's Leap lie behind a stone wall, through a gate.

According to tradition this is the spot where the battle reached its climax. Percy and his men were being pushed back, while Montagu was urging his men to keep formation and push on. At one point Montagu got ahead of his front line and was momentarily exposed. Percy put the spurs to his horse and dashed forward to attack. If he could kill Montagu, the hastily formed Yorkist army might collapse.

The two large stones that are known as Percy's Leap are supposed to mark the take off and landing points of the great spring made by Percy's war horse as he charged forward. These medieval horses were superbly trained for battle, learning to jink sideways, kick backwards and make sudden darting movements on command. Even so the distance between the stones measures about 30 feet, which is clearly too great for any horse carrying a man in armour.

That is not to say that Percy did not make a last ditch effort to kill Montagu, nor that it did not take place here. Merely that the feat has been exaggerated somewhat. In any case, Percy failed. He was hacked from his horse by the Yorkist infantry.

Seeing their leader go down, the Lancastrians lost all will to fight. They fled up into the hills, heading north away from the Yorkists. Again, Montagu did not allow his men to pursue. Not only did he have the task of clearing the battlefield and caring for the wounded to deal with, but he still had the duty of getting the ambassadors safely into Scotland. He wanted to march quickly for he did not know what other surprises his enemies might have in store.

Sir Ralph Percy was still breathing as the victorious Yorkists moved over the field gathering up any weapons or armour that could be salvaged. The young knight was clearly dying, but Montagu ordered that he be made as comfortable as possible. a priest would have been found and the stricken man was asked if he had anything to say before going to meet his maker.

Percy nodded. 'I have saved the bird in my bosom,' he gasped. Then he died.

As famous last words go, this was enigmatic to say the least. Some historians have speculated that Sir Ralph Percy was referring

Left: The gate that gives access from the A697 to Percy's Leap. The site is now surrounded by a protective stone wall but on the day of the battle this was all open grazing land. Their retreat became a rout at about this spot. Right: Percy's Leap. According to legend the dying Percy leapt his horse between these two stones as his enemies closed in upon him. The distance of 30 feet makes this an impressive feat of horsemanship.

to his steadfast loyalty to King Henry VI, but in truth we cannot know what was passing through the mind of this dying man as he lay in great pain.

Having cleared the battlefield, and arranged for the burial of the dead, Montagu continued north to deliver the ambassadors to Scotland. But he knew the chances were that he and his men would have to face the Lancastrians again when they returned this way to England.

12. HEXHAM
1464

Distance:	1¾ miles.
Terrain:	There is a hill to be negotiated on this walk, but it is neither steep nor high. The majority of the walk is over surfaced lanes, with one stretch through woodland where the footpath has a firm surface.
Public Transport:	Hexham is well served by buses and rail, but no public transport link runs to the battlefield itself.
Parking:	Very limited parking space beside the bridge at Linnels where the walk begins and ends.
Refreshments:	No refreshment facilities on this walk, though both pubs serving meals and shops selling snacks and soft drinks can be found in Hexham, two miles to the north-west up the B6306.

After fleeing the field at Hedgeley Moor, Lord Hungerford and Lord Roos gathered their scattered men and headed for the main Lancastrian base at Bamburgh Castle. Here the poor, simple-minded King Henry VI lived as if he were still king over all England, rather than merely commanding a few isolated garrisons and a few thousand men.

Queen Margaret, Henry's wife and the main strength of his opposition, was in Europe trying to drum up support, so the command of Lancastrian forces at this time was in the hands of the Henry Beaufort, the Duke of Somerset. Somerset had originally been a Lancastrian, but in 1462 had recognised the reality of Edward IV's rising power and switched allegiance to the Yorkist side. Edward had showered Somerset with favours, keen to ensure the loyalty of the rich and powerful Beaufort family. Despite this, at Christmas 1463 Somerset slipped away from court and rode north to Bamburgh to

▷ The Devil's Water at
Linnels. Although the stream
itself is neither strong nor deep,
it has steep, high banks that make
it a formidable obstacle.

▽ The Linnel's Bridge. This is
a later reconstruction, but its
narrow width gives a good idea
of the bottleneck that the bridge
would have formed for an army
attempting to cross the stream
here.

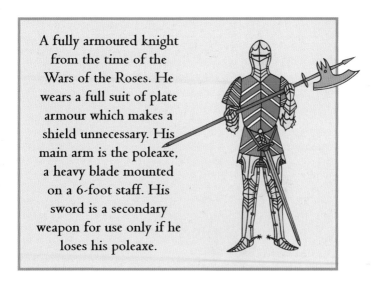

A fully armoured knight from the time of the Wars of the Roses. He wears a full suit of plate armour which makes a shield unnecessary. His main arm is the poleaxe, a heavy blade mounted on a 6-foot staff. His sword is a secondary weapon for use only if he loses his poleaxe.

declare for the Lancastrians again. Edward was furious that a man who had sworn a holy oath of loyalty had betrayed him.

Somerset already knew that the Yorkists were gathering a siege army including modern cannon to move against the Lancastrian castles in the north. Learning of the death and defeat of Sir Ralph Percy at Hedgeley Moor, Somerset decided that the only course open to him was to march south-west to try to link up with Lancastrian supporters in Cheshire, Wales and Gloucestershire. He dragged King Henry with him and on the evening of 14 May put the king behind the secure defences of Bywell Castle before moving on with the army towards Hexham. He did not reach the town before nightfall, so he camped beside the stream known as Devil's Water for the night.

Having completed his task of delivering the ambassadors to do their vital business of negotiating after the fight at Hedgeley Moor, the Yorkist commander Lord Montagu had returned to his main base at Newcastle. Some of the men who had joined him for the march to Scotland had gone home, but he had been reinforced by Lord Greystoke and Lord Willoughby with their retainers. Both these lords had been Lancastrians, but had switched allegiance to Edward IV two years earlier. Given the defection of Somerset, Montagu may not have entirely trusted these new arrivals, but he needed their men.

Montagu's scouts informed him that Somerset and Henry had left Bamburgh, heading south-west on 12 May. Knowing that this was the last Lancastrian army in the field, Montagu realised that its defeat was imperative. If King Henry could be captured the war could be brought to a speedy end. Montagu set off up the valley of the Tyne as soon as he heard the news.

As dusk fell on 14 May the Yorkists marched past Bywell Castle on the south bank of the river. They were seen by Henry and the men with him. Having seen that the main Lancastrian army was not at Bywell, Montagu hurried past unaware that Henry was in the castle.

We don't know where Montagu and his men camped that night, but they were up two hours before dawn to hurry west hoping to catch up with Somerset and, as they thought, Henry before they got to Cheshire.

THE WALK

1. From the bridge over the Devil's Water stream at Linnels, walk south-east along the B6306.

To your left on the south side of the stream spread flat meadows. It was here that Somerset, Roos and Hungerford were camped with their men. In 1464 there was a narrow bridge over the Devil's Water where the modern bridge stands. About half a mile downstream was

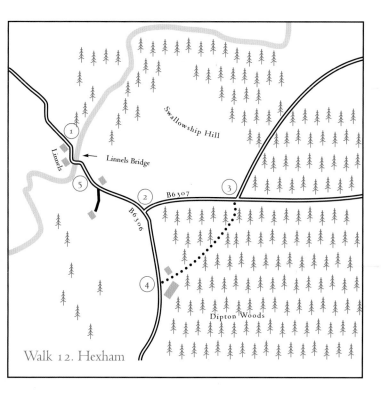

Walk 12. Hexham

a ford, now hidden among the woods that blanket the slopes of Swallowship Hill. As the cold light of dawn started to spread over the hills to the east, the camp began to stir as the men raked out camp fires and prepared to eat breakfast.

The Lancastrian army consisted of about 2,500 men. Of these around 1,500 were men of Hungerford and Roos who had fled from the Battle of Hedgeley Moor almost without striking a blow. It must be assumed that Somerset did not trust these men not to repeat their actions if a battle were to take place. In any case, Somerset had with him 500 of his own men, whom he did trust. There were also some

Somerset's camp ground seen from the B6306 just east of Linnel's Bridge. The Lancastrians were camped here oblivious to how close the advancing enemy were as dawn broke.

Looking north from Somerset's position towards the hill over which the Yorkist army appeared at first light. The main assault was delivered down this road and across the fields on either side.

500 other Lancastrians brought from Bamburgh and commanded by Sir Humphrey Neville, another Lancastrian who had pledged loyalty to Edward of York only to return to his original allegiance.

2. Continue along the B6306 to the junction with the B6307. Turn left and after about 300 yards find a footpath on the right leading into the Dipton Woods.

It was about here that Montagu emerged from Dipton Woods to see the Lancastrian army camped below him in the valley. Montagu had with him about 4,000 men, though over a third of these were retainers of Willoughby and Greystoke. Like Somerset, he was going into battle unable completely to trust a sizeable proportion of his own army. Unlike Somerset, Montagu had an army that was fully armed and ready for action. He decided to take maximum advantage.

Montagu ordered the army to shake itself out of the column in which it had been marching and immediately form up a conventional battle line. He kept his own men with him here, but seems to have sent Greystoke off to the south-west. His job was to come down to the Devil's Water to the south of Somerset's camp and block his retreat in that direction. Greystoke and his men would have marched roughly along the route of the footpath, this section of the hill being rapidly taken up by Montagu's men as they deployed into line. Willoughby's men were probably on his right.

3. Take the footpath through the woods to emerge out of the trees beside a garden nursery on the B6306.

This point was where the left wing of Montagu's men would have been positioned when fully deployed. They were formed up on the hill looking down towards Somerset's camp. The blocking force of

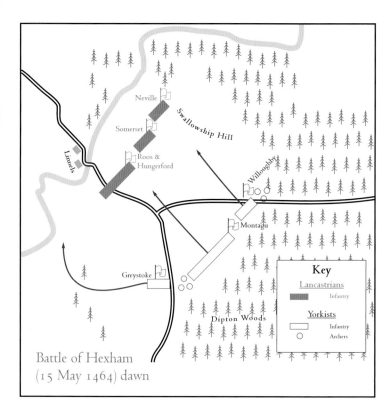

Battle of Hexham
(15 May 1464) dawn

Greystoke would have continued west over what are now open fields
to come down to the stream that lies about a mile distant.

At this date it was usual for English armies to fight almost exclusively on foot, a trend that had been gathering pace since the 1340s.
Knights were encased in complete suits of plate armour that covered
the entire body. Such armour was vulnerable only to crushing blows
from heavy hand-held weapons or to extremely lucky arrowstrikes on
visor or between joints. Most knights suffered more from exhaustion
and heavy bruising than actual wounds. Men-at-arms wore less

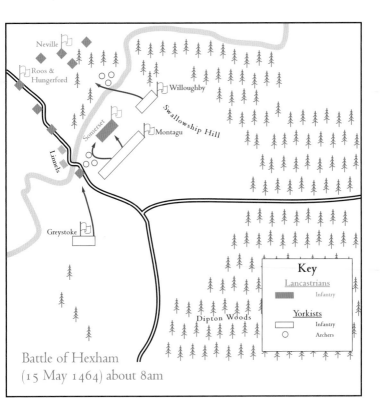

Battle of Hexham
(15 May 1464) about 8am

complete armour, but nevertheless fought alongside the knights. There
were numbers of men called prickers or foreriders, cavalry wearing light
armour who scouted on campaign and guarded flanks in battle. They
often dismounted to fight on foot, as they seem to have done at
Hexham. All armies had considerable numbers of archers. These men
habitually wore metal helmets and some form of body armour.

Montagu would probably have followed conventional tactics by
putting his archers on his flanks and his armoured infantry in the
centre. Then he set off down the hill.

Willoughby led the Yorkist right wing down this slope as the battle opened. He charged from right to left, with Montagu on his left wing moving over the fields in the foreground of the photo.

4. Walk down the B6306 towards Linnels Bridge.

This was the route taken by Montagu's left wing. By this time Somerset had seen the advancing enemy and was getting his men in to position. It seems that there was not enough time for knights and men-at-arms to get fully armoured before they had to take up position. Almost certainly the Lancastrian army drew up in front of their camp in the order in which they had slept. The men of Roos and Hungerford were on the Lancastrian right, in front of the bridge. Somerset's own men were in the centre. Those led by Neville were on the left, in front of the ford.

As they advanced, the Yorkist archers paused to shower the Lancastrians with arrows. The Yorkist knights and men-at-arms did not stop their advance, but continued down the hill at a steady

Somerset and his men made their final stand in this field on the north bank of the stream. By this time both flanks of the Lancastrian army had given way and Somerset's men were on their own.

walk, shouting their battle cries.

The casualties inflicted by the arrows shot by Montagu's flanking archers fell most heavily on the Lancastrian flanks. As the Yorkist infantry got close to the enemy, both wings of the Lancastrian force fled. The men of Roos and Hungerford raced for the bridge, though it was so narrow that not all of them got across before Montagu's men were among them with sword and axe. Neville's men were luckier, splashing over the ford and getting away in large numbers.

With the enemy wings disposed of, Montagu could turn on Somerset himself and his 500 heavily armed infantry. With their backs to the river, there could be little real prospect of escape for the Lancastrians. They fought hard for some time, but when Somerset went down their morale collapsed and the survivors fled. Most did not make it, either being cut down by the Yorkists or drowning in the river.

5. Return to Linnels Bridge where the walk began. It was here that Montagu himself paused in his moment of victory.

Montagu was ordering his foreriders to give chase over the river towards Hexham, when the wounded and dazed Somerset was thrown down before him. Montagu was in no mood to be merciful to the nobleman who had broken his sacred oath. He had Somerset roughly bundled aside to be held at swordpoint along with other prisoners. Montagu was desperate to find King Henry. He sent riders out in all directions to hunt down the fugitives, giving orders that every man killed or captured was to be studied closely. The bodies of the fallen on the field were likewise stripped of helmets and their faces inspected. it was not unknown for important personages such as Henry to be disguised if the prospect of capture seemed likely.

It was soon clear that Henry was not to be found. Montagu by this time was in Hexham itself. He had his prisoners dragged before him one by one. Any Lancastrian who had previously been captured only to return to the field after being let go was not even allowed to speak before being hustled in to the town square for instant execution. Somerset and some two dozen others died in less than an hour. Roos and Hungerford were captured next day and likewise beheaded. The remainder were marched off to Newcastle to await the decision of King Edward as to their fate.

Although the walk ends at Linnels Bridge, Hexham is only a short drive away. There is much to see in the town, including the Abbey and Moot Hall which stood here in 1464 – and the fatal Market Place, now a busy shopping area.

13. BAMBURGH
1464

Distance:	3½ miles.
Terrain:	This bracing coastal walk is mostly over relatively flat ground and well maintained paths, though there is one low hill to be negotiated.
Public Transport:	Travelsure bus route 411 from Berwick.
Parking:	On-street parking in Bamburgh and a car park opposite the castle entrance, where the walk begins and ends.
Refreshments:	A pub and a hotel, both serving meals in Bamburgh.

The crushing defeat at Hexham and ruthless executions that followed served to destroy the Lancastrian cause in northern England, the last bastion of their hopes. A few days after the battle the Lancastrian knight Sir William Tallboys was discovered hiding in a coal mine together with a vast quantity of gold and silver coin – the main treasure of the Lancastrians.

Edward IV, Yorkist King of England, came north to accept the surrenders of those now willing to come to terms, while his cousin and leading commander the Earl of Warwick took the Yorkist army to overcome those who were not. One by one the Lancastrian castles surrendered to Warwick who, on Edward's insistence, was offering generous terms of surrender. Only Sir Ralph Grey, who had betrayed Edward more than once, was exempted from such offers of peace. And all across the north of England Yorkist scouts, soldiers and agents searched for the fugitive King Henry VI, who had not been seen or heard of since leaving Bywell Castle the day after the Battle at Hexham.

In June Warwick and his army appeared before Bamburgh Castle.

Bamburgh Castle from the main car park. Most of the defences are those that stood here at the time of the siege, though the interior of the castle was almost entirely rebuilt in the later ninteenth century to form a comfortable home.

THE WALK

1. From the car park at the north of the village, cross the B1340 and climb up a steep lane to approach the main gates to Bamburgh Castle.

It was here that Warwick's herald rode to shout his terms of surrender up to the soldiers of the garrison. As at the castles of Dunstanburgh, Bywell, Alnwick and Langley they were generous. If the castle surrendered immediately the lives of all within would be spared. Those who had previously sworn allegiance to Edward, but had betrayed him faced imprisonment, but nothing

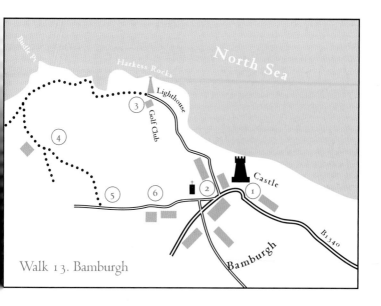

Walk 13. Bamburgh

worse. Others could expect to be fined a sum depending on their wealth and status before being released. Even the Scots and French soldiers known to be in Bamburgh would be allowed to go home. Most urgently, Warwick wanted to know if Henry was in Bamburgh or not.

The garrison commander was Sir Ralph Grey, who knew he could expect no mercy, and he contemptuously refused the offer.

Warwick's herald next tried threats. He declared that his master was as determined to take Bamburgh as had been the Greeks to take Troy and that, like them, he was prepared to sit down for a seven year siege if he had to do so. Moreover, because King Edward wanted Bamburgh intact to guard against Scottish raids in the future, he had decided to execute one man of the garrison for every stone of the defences that was damaged in the coming siege. Unless surrender was agreed to before nightfall.

The main gate to Bamburgh stands on its southern side. It was here that the garrison defied the calls to surrender – at least at first.

Bamburgh Castle from the north as seen from the lane leading to the golf course. At the time of the siege small ships could land on the beach to resupply the castle.

The lighthouse on Harkess Rocks. This squat structure has long been a feature of navigation along England's east coast.

Night fell and there was no surrender.

2. From the castle gates, return down the drive, then turn right to walk west along Front Street to the junction with the road known as The Wyndings to the right.

Once it was clear that Grey was not going to surrender, Warwick settled down to a siege. He brought up the royal siege guns, that had been laboriously dragged from London by teams of oxen averaging barely 12 miles a day. The largest of these were the great iron guns named 'Newcastle' and 'London'. There was an equally large bronze gun named 'Dijon', as well as two smaller iron guns named 'Edward' and 'Richard'.

Nobody is entirely certain where these guns were located, but the pattern of damage sustained by the castle would seem to indicate that at least one of the larger guns fired from this direction, and may have been located at or near this road junction. This was certainly within range of such guns, allowing accurate fire at the curtain walls.

3. Walk north along The Wyndings to pass a row of houses and cross a stream. Beyond the stream the road becomes a narrow lane that leads to a squat lighthouse on the right.

The lighthouse stands on Harkess Rocks, a craggy bluff overlooking the North Sea. During the siege, Warwick maintained a guardpost here to watch the sea approaches to Bamburgh Castle. There was no harbour at Bamburgh, but the sandy beach was ideal for a rowing boat to be beached. It was a continual worry for Warwick that Margaret might return from Europe with a hired army of mercenaries, and land reinforcements at Bamburgh. Alternatively, a single boat could put in to whisk away Henry, if he were indeed inside the walls.

4. Continue past the lighthouse. At a golf clubhouse the track passes through a gate and becomes a mere path hugging the coast. Just after the coast turns south-west to enter Budle Bay a second path veers off to the left over a low hill and towards a cottage. Follow this path, passing the cottage on your right. Beyond the cottage bear left and continue until the path emerges on to a lane, Radcliffe Road, by way of a stile and flight of steps.

5. Turn left along Radcliffe Road. After about 200 yards you will find a cluster of houses on the right of the road.

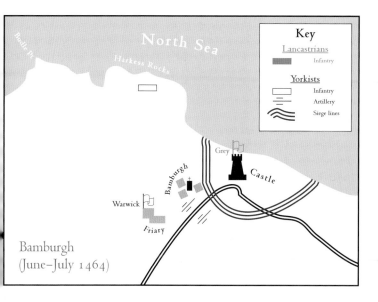

Bamburgh
(June–July 1464)

These houses were built in the 1970s inside the barns and outbuildings of a farm which had, in turn, been converted from the ruins of Bamburgh Friary. In 1464 the Friary was an impressive building in its own right with precincts fortified against Scottish raiders and including a church, cloisters and library. As the only comfortable stone building – apart from the castle – for miles around the Friary was undoubtedly Warwick's headquarters during the siege. If you look carefully you will be able to pick out the older stone walls of the Friary among the more recent building.

It was here, on the morning of 10 July, that a messenger came running to find Warwick with the exciting news that the Lancastrians were offering to surrender. Warwick grabbed his weapons and ran up what is now Radcliffe Road, past the heavy guns to the gates where a knight stood ready to parley.

The walk goes over the hill in the background as it leaves the golf course and bends around to head back towards Bamburgh.

The Friary, a modern housing development that incorporates the ruins of the medieval friary that served as Warwick's headquarters during the siege.

6. Return up Radcliffe Road, past the junction with The Wyndings to follow Warwick's footsteps to the main gates and so to the start of the walk.

The knight waiting for Warwick was not Sir Ralph Grey but Sir Humphrey Neville of Brancepath, his second in command. Sir Humphrey offered to open the gates of the castle to Warwick instantly, but only on the generous terms that had been offered at the start of the siege. In particular Sir Humphrey wanted assurances that his own life would be spared.

Keen to end the business, Warwick agreed. The gates were opened and in marched the Yorkists. They found that a cannonball had struck the roof of the Captain's Lodge (now the souvenir shop) and brought the ceiling crashing down on top of Sir Ralph Grey who had been sleeping inside. Sir Humphrey had promptly taken advantage of his commander's misfortune to come to terms. Grey, it turned out, had been only concussed and had suffered no serious injuries. He was taken prisoner and marched off to Doncaster for trial and execution.

Warwick and his men were disappointed to find that Henry was not within Bamburgh after all. Three days later four 'merchants' in Clitheroe, Lancashire, were thought to be behaving oddly by Sir William Cantelow, a dedicated Yorkist. He seized their groom, one John Livesey, who promptly offered to betray his masters for £7 in cash. Cantelow agreed and so was able to ambush the men as they forded the Ribble just outside town. He thought he had caught Sir Richard Tunstall and Dr Thomas Manning, both of them wanted Lancastrians from the household of Queen Margaret. So he had, but one of the other men turned out to be the elusive King Henry.

Henry was taken to London where he was put into comfortable, but securely guarded chambers. He was allowed servants and fine

The beautiful parish church of Bamburgh has one of the finest chancels in the county. It is also home to the grave of Grace Darling, a daughter of the keeper of Longstone Lighthouse who in 1838 helped her father rescue survivors of the SS Forfarshire after that shipped was wrecked off the coast.

clothes, but contact with the outside world was forbidden. Henry found solace in study and religion, making no attempt to regain his throne. Edward left him alone, but Queen Margaret was still at large. The Wars of the Roses would continue, though they did not bother Northumberland again.

14. NORHAM
1513

Distance:	3¼ miles.
Terrain:	This gentle riverside walk is a pleasant one over paths with good surfaces and village lanes. There is only a short stretch of difficult terrain, which can be avoided, and one flight of steps to negotiate.
Public Transport:	Munros of Jedburgh bus route 67 from Berwick.
Parking:	On-street parking in Norham.
Refreshments:	A pub in Norham village that serves meals and a bakers selling tasty snacks and soft drinks.

In the spring of 1513 all Europe trembled on the edge of war. Aragon, Venice, England and the Holy Roman Empire had formed a league with the Pope against France, which had invaded northern Italy and was becoming perhaps the most powerful state in Europe.

The war began when King Henry VIII of England landed a large army at Calais, then owned by England, and invaded France. He crushed the French force sent to stop him, then captured the cities of Terouenne and Tournay. King Louis XII of France had for some months been urging King James IV of Scotland to distract Henry by invading England. France and Scotland were, after all, bound by the 'Auld Alliance', an anti-English understanding that dated back generations but had no precise form.

James had been reluctant to act for several reasons. First was that the early years of his reign had been taken up with repairing the damage to the Scots economy and society caused by years of civil war. He had only just managed to get things sorted out and had no wish to risk it all by a war with England. He was, moreover,

Norham Bridge. Built in the nineteenth century this bridge is now the main crossing point between England and Scotland along the Tweed between Berwick and Coldstream.

The Tweed at Norham is deep and fast flowing, making this a difficult obstacle to an army. King James of Scotland needed to capture Norham Castle to secure his line of retreat before advancing to Flodden.

married to Henry's sister. James had been happy enough to accept French military advisors to help him raise, equip and train a royal army that would be loyal to himself and permanently on call to help him deal with troublesome nobles. He even had some 5,000 French soldiers in Scotland led by Count d'Aussi. Although he promised repeatedly to attack England, he did nothing.

Driven to desperation by the English attack, Louis sent a ship to Scotland on board were 14,000 French crowns, a considerable sum of cash, plus a letter from Queen Anne of France. The letter was politely phrased, but its message was clear. 'I give you this money,' Queen Anne concluded, 'to pay for an army. I beseech you to come just three feet into England for my sake.' Such a blatant prod to his military reputation – and from a woman at that – was designed to goad James in to action. James, duly goaded, acted.

On 11 August James declared war on England. He demanded an apology and cash payment to compensate him for the death of a Scottish government official who had been killed during a border clash some years earlier and about whom most people had long forgotten. Eleven days later James marched over the border at Coldstream.

The army which James IV led into England was enormous by the standards of the time, about 40,000 fighting men in all. The royal summons had gone out some weeks earlier to all of Scotland. The borderers sent large numbers of reivers armed as lightly armoured cavalry. The Highlands and the Western Isles sent clansmen clad in plaid and carrying their traditional weapons of sword and shield. The Lowlands supplied men equipped with spear, sword and shield. James himself led his royal army. He also brought with him d'Aussi and the 5,000 Frenchmen.

Significantly for what was to follow, James dragged over the Tweed at Coldstream his artillery train. The Scottish Master Gunner, Robert Borthwick, had spent the previous two years buying guns, gunpowder and balls from the finest gunsmiths in Europe. In 1513 his pride and joy were the Seven Sisters, seven guns bought in Flanders that were mounted on carriages able to traverse open fields and which could, therefore, be used in battle. He also had the formidable siege gun Mons Meg, which was clumsily unwieldy but was able to smash stone walls to fragments.

James was well aware that previous attacks into England had foundered when the English ambushed the Scots as they returned. He was therefore determined to fight whatever army the English sent against him before advancing south to plunder and loot. He also decided to keep more than one route back to Scotland open behind him.

The first route was to be back via Coldstream, the second was to be across the Tweed at Norham. The ford here was the only crossing point that could be used by an army supply train between Berwick and where the River Till ran into the Tweed from the south. It was a strategic crossing point of the first order.

James arrived in front of Norham Castle on 25 August.

THE WALK

1. Find Norham bridge, which lies 400 yards west of Norham village where the B6470 crosses the Tweed.

In 1513 there was no bridge, but a ford the exact site of which has been lost. There was little the English garrison could do to stop James and his troops crossing the ford, nor did they intend to do so. Faced by such overwhelming numbers, the garrison task was to sit tight until the Scots army had marched on, then sally out to attack any Scottish supply wagons, stragglers or messengers that came their way. They might even break down the ford to stop it

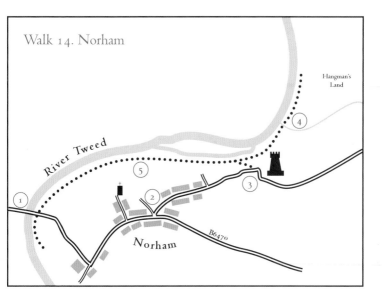

Walk 14. Norham

Hangman's Land

River Tweed

Norham

B6470

being used by the Scots when they tried to cross back into Scotland.

James crossed the Tweed with part of his army by way of this ford and occupied Norham. Having settled in and sent scouts galloping south to watch for any English force in the area, James sent a herald up to the gates of Norham Castle to demand its surrender on generous terms.

2. Leave the bridge walking alongside the B6470 and follow the road into Norham village. The Scottish army camped in and around the village. In the village centre visit the church which has changed little since the time of the siege. James worshipped here during his stay. Leaving the church, continue along the B6470 to the village green, marked by a clock tower, then turn left along Castle Street, signposted to the castle. Where the road jinks to the right, what was in 1513 the main

Left: The church at Norham contains interesting monuments and remains much as it stood during the siege of 1513. Right: The curious clocktower on Norham green that marks where the walk bears to the left off the B6470, the village high street.

entrance to the castle will be seen in front of you. The castle is open to the public during the summer months and is well worth a visit. The modern tourist entrance is about 200 yards to the right of the medieval main gate.

It was here that James's herald stood to shout his master's terms to the English defenders. The garrison, knowing their duty, refused. They had, in any case, been studying the Scottish army. It was large, of that there was no doubt, but they could see no artillery. Norham was a famously strong castle that had not fallen to the Scots for generations and had been recently strengthened. No doubt the garrison felt confident they could hold out.

3. Just before the medieval entrance to the castle find a footpath leaving the road to the left. Follow this footpath

Norham Castle from the south. The arch in the foreground formed the main gate in 1513, but proved impregnable to the Scottish cannon.

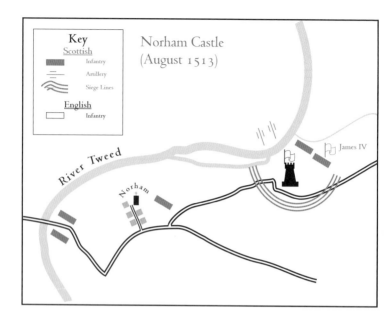

down to the river. Turn right along a path that runs beside the river and has the towering castle walls to the right.

Look across the river to the left. The broad, flat meadow on the far side was where James deployed his nasty surprise for the garrison of Norham. The day after the garrison refused to surrender, the Scottish artillery began to arrive. James put them on this meadow north of the river. From there they were within easy range of the castle, but safe from any sally by the garrison. On the third day the cannon opened fire, Mons Meg hurling its mighty balls over the river with accuracy.

That night one of the garrison slipped over the walls and hurried to James's camp. Apprehended by guards, the man said that he wanted to help the Scots and was taken to see James. The man

The main keep of Norham Castle. In 1318 it had held out against the Scottish army of Robert the Bruce for over a year, standing firm again in 1322. By 1513 it was seriously out of date, but had been surrounded by modern, if not yet complete, defences.

The Tweed at Norham Castle. The castle stands atop the slope to the right, while King James positioned his artillery on the flat meadow to the left of the river.

The small wooden bridge that carries the walk over the stream that falls in to the Tweed just east of the tall cliff on which stands Norham Castle.

quickly told James that the strengthening of one section of wall had not been completed and that it was therefore vulnerable to gunfire. He promised to point out the section to the Scottish gunners in return for a hefty cash payment. James agreed and sent the man over the river to aid his gunners with their aiming.

On the sixth day of the siege the north-eastern corner of the walls of Norham Castle collapsed, just as the traitor had foretold. The Scottish infantry were drawn up ready to attack. In accordance with the useages of war, James summoned the garrison to surrender one last time before ordering the assault. Knowing that they could not hold out, and that they would be killed if the assault went ahead, the garrison surrendered. James spared their lives and bundled the men north of the border into captivity, as was usual.

Beyond the footbridge the path, part of the long distance walk that runs along the Tweed, climbs steeply and becomes unsurfaced. The notorious Hangman's Land lies on top of the slope to the right of the photo.

Meanwhile the traitor came hurrying to find James and claim his reward.

4. Continue over a stile and along the riverside path to where it crosses a small stream by way of a wooden footbridge. The path then climbs steeply and becomes rather uneven and slippery in wet weather. Continue as far along it as you care to.

The meeting between the English traitor and James took place here. The traitor claimed his cash reward. James pulled a pocket of gold coins from his belt and tossed it to the grinning Englishman. Then James ordered the man's immediate execution, declaring that he always kept his promises, but could not abide a traitor.

The walk returns to Norham Bridge along the banks of the Tweed. This is the most gentle and in many ways enjoyable stretch of this walk.

The field north of this little stream is known as Hangman's Land to this day.

Leaving behind a small force to set fire to Norham Castle to make it useless to the English, James set out to attack the castles that guarded the crossing points over the Till: Etal, Ford and Chillingham.

5. Turn back along the riverside path and follow it back to the bridge where the walk began.

15. FLODDEN
1513

Distance:	6¼ miles.
Terrain:	This long walk is mostly over surfaced lanes and tracks, though the climb up to the hill that dominates the battlefield is on an unsurfaced footpath that climbs steeply and can be slippery after rain.
Public Transport:	Branxton is served by Glen Valley Tours bus route 267 from Berwick.
Parking:	On-street parking in Branxton and limited parking in a layby beside the battle monument, where the walk begins and ends.
Refreshments:	A hotel at Point 3 on the walk that serves meals and snacks.

After capturing and burning the hitherto impregnable castle of Norham to secure a second crossing point over the River Tweed, King James IV of Scotland continued his invasion of England by moving against the castles of Etal, Ford and Chillingham to secure crossing points over the River Till. Having seen how easily James's modern artillery had smashed the walls of Norham, the garrisons of the three castles surrendered without a fight. By the end of August, James had completed the first phase of the planned invasion.

The second phase of the Scottish plan called for the English to retaliate. James did not want to make the same mistakes as earlier invaders of England and push too far south raiding before dealing with the main English army. James decided to stay close to the border, choose his ground carefully and wait for the English to arrive. There would be plenty of time for looting

△ Bolton Castle in Wensleydale. The English army paused here on its way north. The army camped in the fields around the castle in pouring rain. It was while here that the army ran out of beer, causing great unrest among the soldiers.

▷ Etal Castle. This fortress guarded a key crossing of the River Till, but surrendered without a fight when faced by the artillery of King James of Scotland. The surrender meant that the English army could not cross the river here on its march on 8 September.

Ford Castle. When waiting for the English army to arrive, King James lodged here while his army camped in the surrounding fields.

and pillaging once the English were beaten. He therefore settled down in Ford Castle, with his army camped around him, having already chosen Flodden Hill as the place where he would face the enemy.

That enemy was gathering quickly. Although King Henry VIII had taken a substantial part of the trained soldiers in England to invade France, he had been well aware that the Scots might invade the moment his back was turned. He had, therefore, left a considerable number of trained soldiers in northern England and put his northern nobles on alert to be ready to raise the local forces. The main English fleet was coasting the North Sea in case it was needed.

The English commander was Thomas Howard, Earl of Surrey. At seventy years of age, Surrey was an old man who was unable to sit a horse for more than an hour and who travelled on campaign in a coach. He was, however, the most experienced soldier in England having fought his way through the Wars of the Roses and seen action in France. He was helped by his son, Lord Thomas Howard, who was admiral of the fleet. When news of the Scottish invasion broke, Admiral Howard docked his fleet at Newcastle and landed 1,200 marines whom he led to join his father.

On 3 September Surrey marched out of Alnwick in driving rain to face the Scots. He had with him about 26,000 men. Of these about 8,000 men might be termed professional soldiers, another 10,000 or so trained semi-professionals and the rest local levies. As Surrey advanced he sent his heralds forward to King James. The rituals of challenge and counter-challenge were gone through. On 5 September, when Surrey was camped in the continuing rain at Bolton Castle, the two commanders agreed that they should fight a battle by 9 September, though James would not agree to Surrey's choice of ground beside the Till and Surrey would not agree to James's on Flodden Edge.

On 7 September Surrey arrived at Wooler and sent his scouts out to inspect the Scottish army. Formed up on Flodden Edge and with his prized artillery entrenched overlooking the road, James was in a commanding position. Any attack was doomed to failure. Surrey and his son, the Admiral, consulted their junior commanders. They decided to take an incredible risk.

Because James had not moved further south, the English rightly concluded that he was not going to do so until he had fought them. They could, therefore, afford to leave the road south open. Instead they would march around the Scottish flank to approach Flodden Edge from the north. This would involve crossing the River Till, marching north along its east bank, then recrossing the river at Twizel Bridge to come down on the Scottish rear. If the Scots moved to hold the line of the Till, the flanking move would be

△ The Twizel Bridge over the Till. The English artillery, cavalry and some infantry crossed the river here on the morning of the battle. The rest of the infantry crossed at a ford a mile upstream despite flooding caused by the heavy rain.

▷ The monument at Flodden, dedicated to the dead of both nations. The walk starts and finishes here.

frustrated. Even worse, if the Scots attacked when the English were half on one side of the Till and half on the other a disaster would surely follow. But having promised to offer battle by 9 September there did not seem much choice.

At dawn on 8 September the English army marched out of Wooler, crossed the Till and headed north-east.

For James and his men on top of Flodden Edge, the move was unexpected. They had hoped the English would attack them in their entrenched position. It was still raining, so the English quickly vanished into the gloom. There was a hurried discussion. Some thought the English might be off to invade Scotland by way of Berwick, others that it was a trap to lure the Scots off their hill. James decided to stay where he was, sending out scouts to try to discover what the English were up to.

Late that evening a group of English knights was seen on a small hill beyond the Till. This was the Admiral making sure that the Scots were still on the hill and had not moved towards Twizel Bridge.

Next morning, 9 September, dawned murky and misty. Then the rain began again. Around 9am a Scottish patrol at Twizel Bridge saw the main English army looming up out of the murk. They hurried off to inform King James. In fact only half the English army, plus the artillery, crossed the Till at Twizel under the command of Surrey. The bulk of the English infantry was crossing a mile upstream at the Milfield Ford. The heavy rains of the preceding week meant that this was the only ford that could be used, and even then not by guns, wagons or cavalry.

By around 11am the English army was over the Till and marching south. Between them and the Scots lay the Pallinsburn Bog, then the low Branxton Ridge and finally a steep climb up Branxton Hill to the plateau of Flodden. The rain began to ease, but was still falling as the English reached the northern side of Pallinsburn Bog.

There were only two fords over suitable for horses and artillery, though the infantry could wade over.

THE WALK

1. Find the monument, which lies down a lane about 200 yards west of Branxton Church. The monument stands on a smooth knoll, known as Piper Hill, which forms the western end of the slight Branxton Ridge.

The Admiral got over the bog first and began deploying his men on the western end of the Branxton Ridge as had been agreed the night before. On his right, just south-west of Piper Hill he put 3,000 levies from Cheshire and Lancashire under Lord Edmund Howard, his younger brother. In the centre he put himself with his marines, the Yorkshire militia and others that made up a total of 9,000 men. This formation stretched from in front of Piper Hill almost to in front of the church. On his left in front of the church was Sir Marmaduke Constable with a further 3,000 northern levies.

As the Admiral deployed his men, the vanguard of Surrey's force came trotting up under Lord Dacre. Dacre had 1,500 cavalry, plus some 2,000 archers who fought on foot but had ridden to battle on ponies. The Admiral put Dacre behind his line as a reserve.

The Admiral was probably standing on top of Piper Hill issuing his orders when he saw the ominous sight of the massed ranks of the Scottish army appearing on top of Branxton Hill to his south. It was about 1pm. Fearing the Scots were about to charge down with overwhelming numbers, the Admiral sent a desperate message off to his father urging him to hurry. When Surrey got the message, he was just completing getting his main body of about

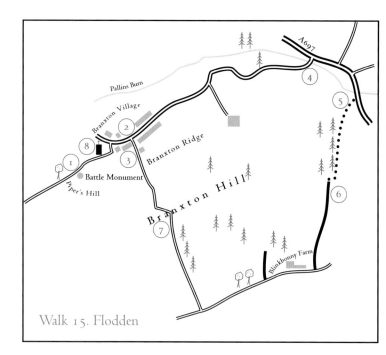

Walk 15. Flodden

5,000 infantry, plus artillery, over the bog. Urging the gunners to follow as quickly as possible, Surrey led his infantry quickly west to form up on Constable's left, in front of Branxton village.

In his haste, Surrey sent a galloper back to his rearguard that was still north of the bog with a garbled order. This told Lord Stanley and his 3,000 infantry merely to hurry over the bog, but gave him no clear orders what to do on the other side.

2. Walk east, back to Branxton church. At the end of the lane, turn right to enter Branxton village. Turn right along a lane beside a phone box. Follow this lane to the top of the slight rise of Branxton Ridge.

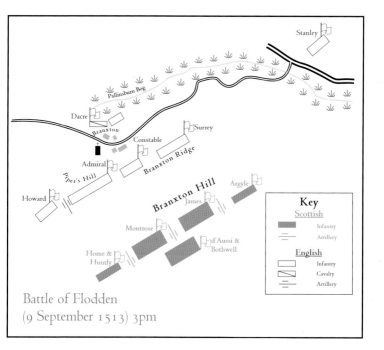

Battle of Flodden
(9 September 1513) 3pm

This was the spot occupied by the right flank of Surrey's division, with Constable to his right. It was here that Surrey put some of his artillery when they came up. The remainder were put immediately south of the church with the Admiral's division. A few of the Scottish cannon had been firing balls down on the English as they deployed. Surrey decided to reply in kind. At about 3pm the English guns opened fire.

At this date field artillery were not particularly accurate at long range. The slow rate of fire, compared to later guns, further diminished their effectiveness. However the noise, fire and smoke were impressive and their ability to inflict even light casualties at long range was novel and unnerving.

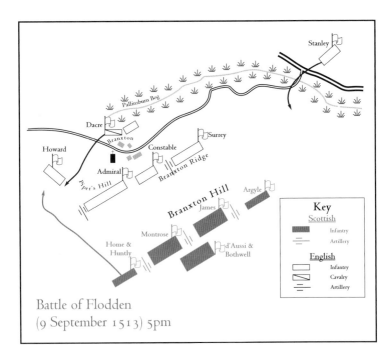

Battle of Flodden
(9 September 1513) 5pm

Key

Scottish

Infantry

Artillery

English

Infantry

Cavalry

Artillery

It would seem that both Surrey and James had very similar plans in mind for the afternoon of 9 September. Both knew that they had promised to offer battle, but neither wanted to do so on the other's terms. James wanted to stay on the strong defensive position of the hilltop and have Surrey attack him. Surrey wanted to stay on his much lower ridge, and lure James down to attack him. The entire afternoon could have passed in ineffective long range gunfire, but it did not.

In drawing up his army, James had paid close attention to the advice of d'Aussi, the French nobleman who had been in Scotland for months giving instruction in modern warfare techniques.

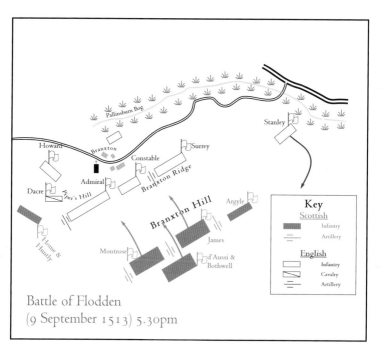

Battle of Flodden
(9 September 1513) 5.30pm

The key tactical innovation brought by d'Aussi was the pike phalanx. This consisted of a solid mass of infantry formed up twelve ranks deep. Each man wore plate armour and was equipped with a 14-foot pike, plus a sword for close combat. The men were trained to stand shoulder to shoulder in ranks that were so close each man could feel the breath of the man behind him. The front four ranks held their pikes horizontally forward to form a continuous hedge of sharp steel points. Those behind held their pikes sloping upward and forward. They were thus ready to step forward to take the place of fallen comrades, while the shafts of their pikes served to deflect incoming arrows.

Formed up in such a phalanx, the infantry would be set in

motion marching forward at a steady pace. So long as the formation was kept tight, and kept moving, it was effectively invulner-
able. The bristling mass of long pikes was impenetrable to an
enemy, while the momentum would simply crush enemy formations. Even if the front ranks balked at closing with the enemy,
the men behind would push on and drive the pikes into the
opposing troops.

The tactic had worked again and again for the Swiss who
invented it, and the French who copied it. But it took a great deal
of skill for every man to march at the same pace, keeping the rigid
close order of the phalanx. D'Aussi and his Frenchmen had been
drilling the Scots lowland infantry for weeks in the tactic.

D'Aussi and James were confident that their newly trained
men could fight well enough in phalanx, but were worried that
they could not manoeuvre as well as they should. In particular the
Scottish pikemen might not be able to turn quickly to face a
flank attack. Fortunately James had with him large numbers of
border reivers, Highlanders and Islanders who were adept at fast,
swirling charges and movement.

The positioning of the Scottish army on top of Branxton Hill
was designed to take advantage of these tactical imperatives. In the
centre, facing the Admiral, Constable and Surrey, were two large
phalanxes of about 8,000 pikemen led by the Earl of Montrose on
the left and James himself on the right. Behind these two was a
third phalanx, again of about 8,000 men led by d'Aussi. It was
made up of the 5,000 Frenchmen plus some 3,000 lowlanders
under the Earl of Bothwell.

To guard the flanks of these phalanxes, James put 5,000
Highlanders under the Earl of Argyle on the right. On the left,
facing towards Howard's division was a force of about 3,000
borderers under Lord Home, plus 2,000 Highlanders under Lord
Huntly.

The view from the Flodden monument looking east. The English army was drawn up in the fields to the right of the church by early afternoon.

The view looking west from Point 3 of the walk. The slope to the left is the lower section of Branxton Hill on top of which the Scottish army was formed. The slighter slope to the right is Branxton Ridge on top of which the English army was positioned.

The entrance to the gully used by Lord Stanley and his men, as seen from the A697, close to the spot where Stanley stood having crossed the bog and before beginning his flanking march that would be so successful. The walk crosses this field and then runs up the hill beside the left hand group of trees.

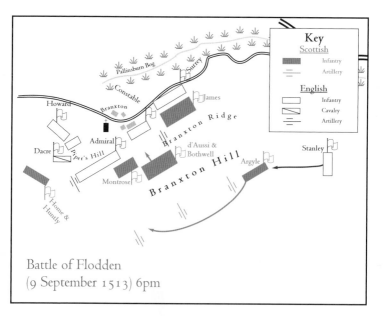

Battle of Flodden
(9 September 1513) 6pm

The disposition was strong and carefully calculated. However, James chose to put himself in the heart of the phalanx that he himself commanded. This made it difficult for him to convey orders to other formations of his army. This was to prove crucial.

By about 4.30pm the rain had ceased. In the clearer visibility and drier conditions the firing of the cannon speeded up and became more accurate. The Scots had the better guns, but the English were the better gunners. Casualties among the Scots, although light, were beginning to mount. It was too much for the poorly disciplined borderers to bear. Led by Lord Home they swept down from the hill to attack Howard's division. The impact of the charge was increased when Huntly's Highlanders piled in. Howard's division gave ground, then retreated. The extreme English right wing collapsed completely, the men fleeing north as

Battle of Flodden
(9 September 1513) 7pm

fast as they could. The formation where Howard himself was, fell
back quickly towards Piper's Hill.

Up on Branxton Hill, James watched with glee as the English
right wing crumpled. When he saw a mass of Highlanders swing
right around the back of Piper's Hill as if about to attack the
Admiral in the rear, James shouted in triumph. He gave the order
for the three phalanxes to march down the hill to attack. It was
about 5pm.

From his position here in front of Branxton village, Surrey
watched the Scots descending the hill in perfect order. It was a
daunting sight for the waiting English. Although they too wore
heavy armour, the English favoured the bill over the Scottish spear
or Swiss pike. The weapon was about eight feet long and carried

both a thrusting spike and a cutting axe blade. In the hands of an expert it was a deadly weapon, but it was considerably shorter than the new-style pikes being used by the Scots. The Scots would be able to hit the English before the English could retaliate.

The two leading Scottish phalanxes reached the bottom of Branxton Hill, then started to climb up the slight slope of Branxton Ridge. Montrose's phalanx had to cross ground broken by hedges and so lost some of its formation before it struck the English line. James's phalanx had no such obstacles and ground on into Surrey's division. The English bills were no match for the pikes, and the English fell back steadily until they reached the road running through Branxton.

3. Return along the lane to Branxton High Street.

In 1513 there were no houses along this section of road, the village being clustered around the church. It was here that the Scottish advance came to a halt. The phalanxes had been successfully stopped, but were still intact. Anxiously, James would have tried to see beyond Surrey's men to find out where the borderers had got to and why they were not yet attacking the English rear.

In fact, while the phalanxes were coming down the hill, the borderers had been defeated by a charge of cavalry led by Lord Dacre from his position behind the Admiral's men. The borderers and highlanders were now regrouping south-west of Piper's Hill. Dacre was on top of Piper's Hill calling up his archers while Howard was trying to regroup his men behind Dacre's cavalry. Effectively the battle had come to a standstill, though the killing continued.

4. Turn right along Branxton High Street. Continue beyond the village as the lane winds through open fields to reach the small stream that is all that is left of the Pallinsburn Bog.

The view north from Point 6 of the walk. The path skirts with wood to join a track heading south.

Lord Stanley, leading the 3,000 men of Surrey's rearguard had just about got his men over the bog and was standing here as James led his phalanxes down the hill. Stanley saw the move, but also saw that Argyle and his Highlanders had not moved. They remained up on Branxton Hill, staring down into the valley below. They were not, however, looking east to where Stanley stood. Stanley could also see that a narrow ravine ran up from the eastern foot of the hill to the rear of Argyle's position.

5. At the end of the lane turn right along the A697. After passing two turnings to the left a footpath leaves the road over a stile to the right. Turn right up this path. As it starts to climb the hill, the path skirts to the left of a small, but dense wood which fills the ravine used by Stanley. It then emerges

on to the hill top only slightly to the south of Stanley's position as he merged from the gully.

As soon as he got on to the plateau, Stanley realised that he had not been seen by the Highlanders. Hurriedly shaking his men into formation, Stanley launched an attack. Starting with a shower of arrows that took a heavy toll on the unarmoured Highlanders, Stanley followed up with a charge at the jog trot by his armoured billmen.

Taken by surprise, shot down by arrows and assaulted by armoured men, the Highlanders fled. They went first west, then poured over the edge of the hill towards their comrades under Huntly west of Branxton.

6. A farm track heads south from the end of the wood. Follow this track to a surfaced lane. Turn right to pass Blinkbonny Farm and a small wood. Then turn right to head north up a lane across the plateau. After about 400 yards the lane reaches the crest of the hill and Branxton village comes into view.

Stanley chased the Highlanders and emerged on to the crest of the hill at this spot. He was able to look down on the main battle raging beneath him. It was the first time that he was able to see what was going on.

To the west he could see Argyle's men joining those of Huntly and Home. The arrival of the defeated men tipped the balance for the borderers. Glancing anxiously at Stanley's men high above, they began drifting away north-west towards Coldstream and the border.

Directly in front of him, Stanley could see the phalanx of d'Aussi and Bothwell coming into action to support that of Montrose which was being pushed back by the divisions of the

Admiral and Constable. Slightly to his right Stanley found himself looking at the unguarded rear of the phalanx led by King James, which was engaged in a brutal fight with Surrey and his men.

Stanley barely paused to consider the situation. He put his men into line with archers on the flanks and went down the hill.

7. Follow down the lane as it descends the hill. Continue north across the shallow valley, up the slope of Branxton Ridge and back to Point 3 on the walk.

Stanley paused here for his archers to pour a withering, close range volley into the unarmoured backs of the Scots, then charged home with his billmen. It was carnage. Unable to turn around with their long pikes, the Scots were hacked to pieces. Those that threw aside their pikes found that their swords were no match for the English bills.

Meanwhile, Lord Dacre left his archers and Howard's infantry to watch the retreating borderers and Highlanders before leading his cavalry on a second charge into the left flank of King James's phalanx. The new blow was too much and the Scottish formation collapsed. So tightly packed were the Scotsman that they could not use their weapons properly as the English closed in for the kill. Only a few dozen of the 8,000 men got away alive.

Seeing the left wing flee and disaster overtaking the king's phalanx, d'Aussi was trying to extricate his own phalanx from the disaster. He was helped by the gathering dusk and by the fact that his Frenchmen were better trained at manoeuvring in formation than the Scots. Taking heavy losses, he managed to pull his formation away to the west, skirting around Piper's Hill.

Night fell with the English in command of the bloodstained battlefield. Next day dawned to reveal d'Aussi with his men and some borderers a mile or so to the north-west. They soon moved

The view from Point 7 of the walk. King James stood here when the battle began, and later Stanley launched his attack from this same spot.

off to Coldstream once they realised that they were alone. It was only when daylight came that the English began to realise the scale of their victory.

King James was dead, and so was a sizeable proportion of the Scottish nobility. Twenty-four earls and senior lords lay dead, as did two abbots, two bishops and the Archbishop of St Andrew's. At least 10,000 non-nobles were also killed, some think as many as 15,000. The English had lost about 2,000 men.

8. Continue back to Branxton High Street. Turn left to find Branxton Church.

In the chancel King James's body was laid in state before being taken to Newcastle to be embalmed. The king's bloodsoaked clothing was packed up and sent to King Henry in France along with the despatch announcing the victory. The body was then taken to London to be displayed to the public before being buried at Sheen in Surrey.

Never again did a Scottish king or noble seek to invade England. The border reivers remained active with their cattle raids, but the days of massed invasions from the north were over.

INDEX